EDWARDIAN STYLE
HAND-KNITTED FASHION
❧ FOR 1/12 SCALE DOLLS ❧

EDWARDIAN STYLE HAND-KNITTED FASHION

❧ FOR 1/12 SCALE DOLLS ❧

Yvonne Wakefield

GUILD OF MASTER CRAFTSMAN PUBLICATIONS

First published 2002 by
Guild of Master Craftsman Publications Ltd
Castle Place, 166 High Street,
Lewes, East Sussex BN7 1XU

Book and cover design:
Wheelhouse Design, Brighton, Sussex
Editor: David Arscott

ISBN 1 86108 241 X

Set in Frutiger and Berkeley

Colour origination by Viscan Graphics (Singapore)
Printed by Kyodo Printing (Singapore)

To my conveyors of sunshine,

Daisy and Ruth

ABBREVIATIONS

k – knit,
p – purl,
st(s) – stitch(es)
st st – stocking stitch, (knit right side rows, purl wrong side rows)
rev st st – reverse stocking stitch, (purl right side rows, knit wrong side rows)
g st – garter stitch, (knit all rows)

mm – millimetres
cm – centimetres
in – inches

rep. – repeat
beg – begin, beginning
tog – together
cont – continue
foll(s) – follow, follows, following
alt – alternate
rem – remain
patt – pattern
dec – decrease
inc – increase

RH – right hand
LH – left hand

RS – right side
WS – wrong side

sl – slip: slip the stitch onto the right hand needle without working it
psso – pass the slipped stitch over the next stitch and off the needle
ybk – take the yarn to the back of the work
tbl – through the back of the loop: work the stitch through the back loop
fbf – front, back, front: work into the front, then the back, then the front of the next stitch to make two new stitches.

[- - -] The instructions contained within square brackets are to be repeated by the number of times stated immediately after the bracket.

Right front/Left front
When a garment piece is described as being left or right in the knitting instructions, it means the wearer's left or right. For example, the 'left front' will be the front on the wearer's left-hand side, and the 'right sleeve' will be the sleeve worn on the right arm.

COMPATIBLE TERMS

cast off	bind off
alternate rows	every other row
tension	gauge
miss	skip
work straight	work even
stocking stitch	stockinette stitch

COMPATIBLE NEEDLE SIZES

British	Continental	American
19	1.00mm	5/0
20	0.90mm	
21		
22	0.75mm	6/0
24	0.60mm	7/0

INCREASING

m1 – make one stitch: pick up the yarn of previous row that is stretched between the needles and knit into the back of it. This method is used when an invisible increase is needed.

yo – yarn over: from the front, take the yarn over the needle to make one new stitch before knitting the next stitch. This method is used to increase one stitch, after a purl stitch and before a knit stitch.

2yo – two yarn over: take yarn twice round needle to make two new stitches.

yrn – yarn round needle: take the yarn from the front, over and round the needle, returning to the front position. This method is used to increase one stitch in between two purl sts.

yfwd – yarn forward: bring the yarn to the front of the work. This instruction is used when an increase is needed between two knitted stitches.

inc into next stitch, last stitch), or inc 1 st (at beginning or end of row): knit into the front, then the back loop of the appropriate stitch.

DECREASING

k2tog – knit 2 together: insert the right hand point into the front loop of the second stitch and then the first stitch on the left hand needle, and knit the two stitches together. This decreases one stitch and produces a slope to the right.

sl1-k1-psso – slip one, knit one, pass the slipped stitch over: slip the next stitch onto right hand needle, knit the next stitch, then pass the slipped stitch over the knitted stitch and off the needle. This decreases one stitch and produces a slope to the left.

ssk – slip 1 stitch knit-wise twice, then, approaching from the left, place the point of the left hand needle into the front loops of the two stitched, and knit them together from this

position. This decreases one stitch and produces a slope to the left, and is rather neater than the above method.

sl2tog-k1-p2sso – slip 2 together, knit 1, pass 2 slip stitches over: place the point of the right hand needle into the loops of the next two stitches as if to knit the two stitches together, but rather than working them, slip them onto the right hand needle. Knit the next stitch, and pass the two slipped stitches over the knitted stitch and off the needle. This makes a very neat double decrease that places the centre stitch neatly over the top of the other two.

dec at beg or end of row – knit together the first two or the last two stitches of the row.

Britannia rules

March 8, 1906. A Government Blue Book, published today, reveals that the British Empire now occupies a fifth of the globe, with a total population of 400 million – three quarters of them living in India.

More than 3 million square miles have been added to the Empire in the last 25 years.

Contents

Pope is not amused

January 8, 1904 The Pope has made an attack on the low-cut evening gowns now in fashion, saying that no woman who wishes to be thought a good Catholic should wear one in the presence of cardinals or other Church dignitaries. Some wives of diplomats are threatening to stay at home rather than comply.

The Edwardian Age

1901

Edward VII succeeds to the throne on
the death of his mother, Queen Victoria
First British submarine launched
Marconi sends radio signal from
Cornwall to Newfoundland

1902

Second Boer War ends
Order of Merit established
Edison invents electric storage battery

1903

Motor car speed limit set at 20mph
Emmeline Pankhurst founds suffragettes
Wright brothers make their first flight
Ford Motor Company founded

1904

Workers' Educational Association begins
First mainline electric trains in UK
Charles Rolls and Henry Royce agree to
manufacture cars together

1905

Einstein propounds Theory of Relativity
Automobile Association established
Aspirin on sale for the first time
First public cinema shows in London

1906

Liberals win landslide election
Bakerloo and Piccadilly underground
lines open in London
F.G. Hopkins discovers vitamins
Devastating earthquake strikes
San Francisco

1907

Baden-Powell organises first Boy
Scouts camp
Motor racing begins at Brooklands
Florence Nightingale appointed to
Order of Merit

1908

Olympic Games held in London
Ford's first Model T produced in Detroit
W.G. Grace retires from first-class cricket

1909

Old age pensions introduced for
the over-70s
Selfridge's store opens in London
Bleriot makes first cross-Channel flight

1910

Edward VII dies and is succeeded by
his son, George V

Introduction

Well at last it is finished. My first book is complete. I feel as if I have been knitting tiny Edwardian garments for ever. Free time at last: gardening here I come. But what fun it has been, even though I seriously under-estimated the amount of time that I would spend knitting all that lace.

My book does not in any way pretend to be a concise history of fashion, any more than the garment designs pretend to be accurate copies of Edwardian wear. Although many of the patterns are based on real garments or paper patterns of the period, my intention is rather to create a mood and develop a feel for the era in a way that is appropriate to the craft of knitting.

Hand knitting can be a very satisfying creative pastime, and working in miniature provides that extra challenge that some of us need – but please don't forget the fun. If you're not happy using very tiny size 21 needles, then use size 20. The lace or rib may be slightly bigger, but so what? Or perhaps you suddenly realize that there is a mistake 12 rows down in that complicated lace pattern you are in the middle of knitting. Well, does it really matter? I'm sure that many errors can be found in genuine Edwardian hand-wrought lace: leave it, stop worrying, enjoy your task. Everything to do with either knitting or 1/12 scale dolls should be joyous, not arduous.

I do hope that you become inspired to try out these patterns, and that you will derive a great deal of pleasure from your dressed dolls.

Yvonne Wakefield

Materials & methods
MATERIALS AND EQUIPMENT

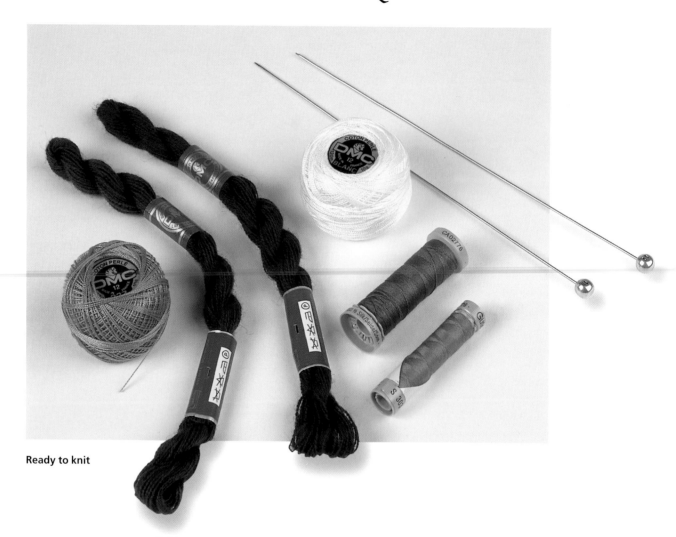

Ready to knit

NEEDLES

Needles size 19 (1.00mm, 5/0), size 20 (0.90mm) and size 21 (0.80mm) have been used throughout the book. If you have problems obtaining the sizes stated, (there is, for instance, no equivalent of British size 20 in America) please see page 128.

YARNS

Four types of yarn are specified. All of them are commonly used for sewing, crochet or embroidery and should be easy to obtain.

Gütermann pure silk thread, a machine sewing thread available in a wide range of colours from haberdashery shops.

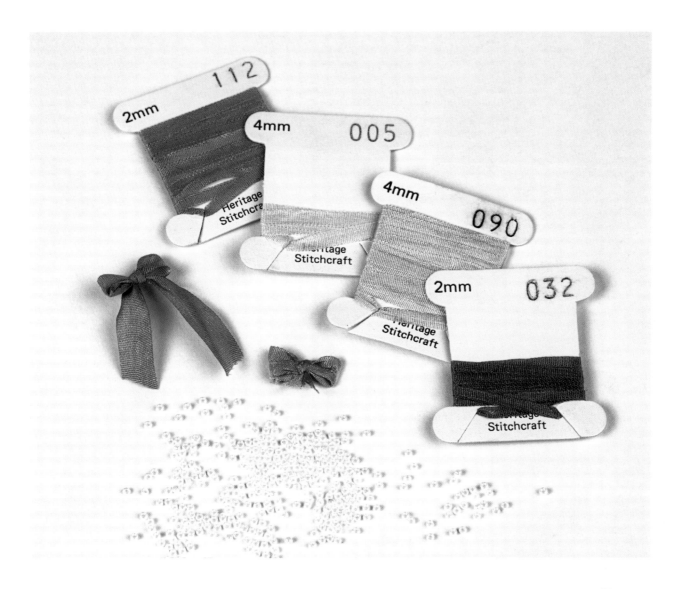

Buttons and bows

Gütermann top stitching thread, a polypropylene thread that is slightly thicker than the silk, producing a thicker, firmer fabric

DMC cotton perlé size 12, a shiny mercerized cotton yarn.

DMC Brode Medicis Laine Tapisserie, a fine pure wool that is slightly hairy and which therefore has a tweed look.

MATERIALS FOR DECORATION

A selection of silk ribbon, 2mm, 4mm, and 7mm wide, will be useful for ruching, making bows and roses, etc.

Very tiny Fairy or Petite embroidery beads can be used for buttons.

USEFUL EQUIPMENT

It is encouraging for beginners to discover that this list is relatively short:

Steam iron: essential for good finishing.

Miniature finishing/ironing board (see page 6). These are readily available from miniaturist suppliers.

Short lengths of small diameter doweling, for steaming sleeves and other tiny bits.

Measuring tape, sharp pointed scissors, sewing needles.

Rose maker and bow maker (sold by most suppliers of miniature haberdashery).

Box of wet hand wipes – really useful when knitting white silk.

SIZES AND MEASUREMENTS

The patterns have been designed to fit the very slim all-porcelain 1/12 scale dolls. Ladies are 5 1/2 inches tall, men 6 inches tall, and all children 4 inches tall.

If your lady dolls are like mine and have nice pert, high, pointed busts, you may like to invest some time in a little surreptitious padding in order to create the low slung mono bosom typical of the fashionable Edwardian woman.

All the patterns have openings or some means of allowing garments to go over heads and arms when dressing the dolls. Some of the openings have button fastenings, while others are stitched up after the doll is dressed. Having proper button openings is not totally satisfactory, as it is virtually impossible to work buttonholes small enough to hold the tiny beads or buttons of the correct scale.

If you want the holes to work you may need to cheat and use a needle and thread to tighten them up a little. When I need to have removable clothes on a doll, I usually miss out the buttonholes and stitch the buttons to the buttonhole band, then invisibly tack the buttonhole and button bands together. I leave a big knot in one end of my thread and a long tail at the other, both ends then being hidden on the underside of the bands. To remove the clothes I just pull the knot and remove the tacking thread.

For skirts, the gathering thread at the waist can be replaced with fine knitting-in elastic.

KNITTING METHODS

Get into shape: the 'S' curve

Since I have assumed that anyone attempting miniature knitting already has good basic knitting skills and knowledge, I have not provided any instruction in knitting techniques. Here, however, are a few tips which you may find useful.

TENSION

Do knit a tension square, and test your tension before knitting a garment.

There is no such thing as a correct tension. The fact of the matter is that some of us knit loosely and some of us knit tightly. In order to obtain the stated sizes you need to adjust either your needle size or the number of rows and stitches used.

ABBREVIATIONS

There is a full list of abbreviations at the front of the book, but to save the frustration of having to keep checking back, where some of the less common ones are used in a pattern they are also listed at the beginning of it.

STOCKING STITCH, CURLING EDGES

When knitting stocking or stockinette stitch, the side edges of the fabric will curl towards the back, making stitching up a bit of a pain. The curl happens because the fabric is unbalanced. When working stocking stitch, both the purl stitches and the knit stitches throw more yarn to the back or (purl) side of the fabric, than to the front or smooth side, causing the imbalance.

If on every purl or wrong side row the second stitch and the last but one stitch are knitted, this will help redress the problem just a little. It's a bit like putting a mini rib at each edge.

KNITTING WITH WHITE YARN

In order to keep the silk thread as clean and white as possible, I found it helpful to take the following precautions.

- When working, keep the spool of yarn in a small plastic freezer or food bag, with an elastic band round the top.
- Place a clean towel or cloth on your knee.
- Keep a pack of wet hand wipes handy, and use them frequently. I use whatever is to hand, including antiseptic kitchen wipes, baby wipes and face cleansers.

SHAPING BY KNITTING SHORT ROWS

Short row knitting is used throughout the knitting instructions to create three-dimensional shape within a piece of knitted fabric. It involves knitting part of a row, turning, then working back, allowing some sections of the knitting to have more rows than others.

Unfortunately, just turning can leave an unsightly hole. Sometimes these small holes are of no consequence (on shoulder shaping, for example, they disappear into the seam), but if you don't want holes the following instructions give one way of avoiding them. The instructions are in two parts: wrapping the stitch and picking up and knitting in the wrap strand.

1 Work the number of stitches stated, but before turning, take the yarn to the other side of the work, slip the next stitch purl-wise, return the yarn to the original side of the work, slip the stitch back onto the LH needle, and turn.

2 Next we have to get rid of the strand of yarn wrapping the stitch, as it is now visible on the right side of the work. Follow the pattern instructions for the garment that you are knitting until you meet the wrapped stitch of the previous row.

On a k row

Work to the wrapped stitch. Insert the point of the RH needle into the loop lying on the RS of

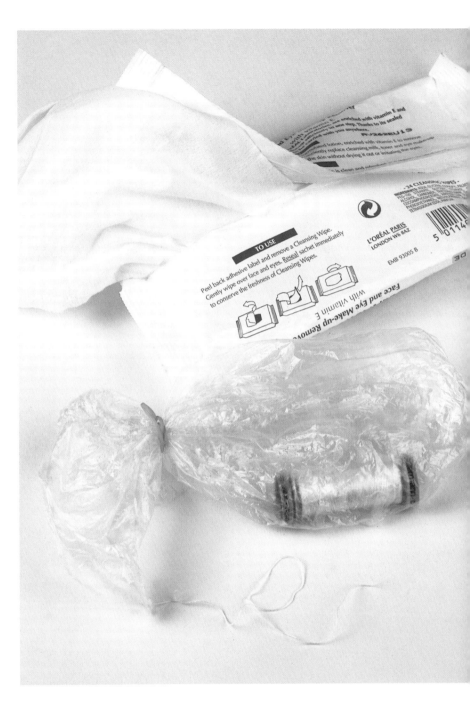

work, from underneath, as if to knit it, then into the wrapped stitch. Now knit together the stitch and the loop.

On a p row

Work to the wrapped stitch. Insert the point of the RH needle, first into the loop lying on the RS of the work, from underneath, as if to purl it, then into the back loop of the wrapped stitch. Now purl together the stitch and the loop.

Whiter than white

FINISHING AND STITCHING UP

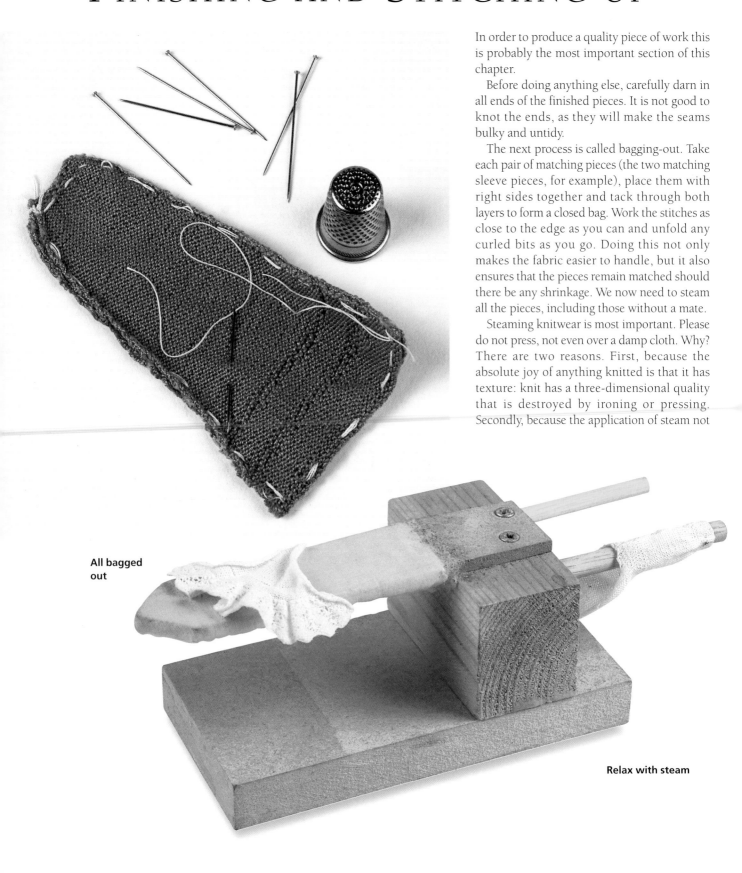

In order to produce a quality piece of work this is probably the most important section of this chapter.

Before doing anything else, carefully darn in all ends of the finished pieces. It is not good to knot the ends, as they will make the seams bulky and untidy.

The next process is called bagging-out. Take each pair of matching pieces (the two matching sleeve pieces, for example), place them with right sides together and tack through both layers to form a closed bag. Work the stitches as close to the edge as you can and unfold any curled bits as you go. Doing this not only makes the fabric easier to handle, but it also ensures that the pieces remain matched should there be any shrinkage. We now need to steam all the pieces, including those without a mate.

Steaming knitwear is most important. Please do not press, not even over a damp cloth. Why? There are two reasons. First, because the absolute joy of anything knitted is that it has texture: knit has a three-dimensional quality that is destroyed by ironing or pressing. Secondly, because the application of steam not

All bagged out

Relax with steam

only relaxes but also changes the structure of the knitted stitch, and this is to the advantage of the fabric quality.

The yarn or thread that we use for knitting is spun in such a way that the molecules lie, more or less, in a straight line. When we knit we force the thread into the lovely curves which form each stitch, much to the distaste of the molecules which would much prefer to remain in their straight line. When we drop a stitch, it can't wait to travel down and become a ladder of straight lines. Steam (heat and moisture) reacts with the molecules, causing them to relax and to sit more happily in their new curved shape. If you try knitting a small square, apply steam by holding the steam iron about two inches above the fabric. Allow the work to dry, and then unravel some of it: you will see quite clearly that the stitches now stay in the curved shape and do not ladder. This is good to remember should you make a mistake and need to unravel some rows to put it right. The stitches will be much easier to pick up if the fabric has been steamed.

So steaming, rather than pressing or ironing, is best for knit. Hold the iron above the fabric without touching it, and try not to handle the fabric until you are sure that it is absolutely dry.

Lace needs to be treated a little differently. To look its best it needs to be stretched. I do this by first spraying the lace with water, then using my fingers to pull it in each direction, stretching it quite firmly. I finish by pulling it into the shape I prefer, making sure that the points or scallops are defined, leaving the lace trim on a towel to dry. I don't block and pin my lace. This might be a great method for doilies or pillow edging, but I find the result too crisp and sharp for use on garments. I prefer a softer, more draping effect.

STITCHING UP

Stitching up can be done using either a back-stitched seam or an over-sewn seam: it's a matter of personal preference. I use both. The over-sewn seam is less bulky but can stretch the fabric if not very carefully worked. On the other hand, if the edges to be stitched are a bit ragged, a back-stitch seam is probably neater.

For garments knitted with the top-stitching thread or the wool, it is easier to use a fine

Stretch it out

sewing thread for stitching up. The top-stitch thread is a bit bulky for seaming, and difficult to thread though the eye of a small needle. The pure wool yarn, though great for knitting, lacks sufficient strength for sewing – pulling it through the fabric will cause it to wear and break as you stitch. Try using a basic machine sewing thread in an appropriate colour.

Edwardian Style

Edward VII was King of Great Britain for a very short time – a little less than ten years. His reign began on the death of his mother, Queen Victoria, in 1901, and it lasted until his own death in 1910. Fashion historians record this brief period as a time of exciting, luxurious style, the like of which has never been repeated. It would be nonsensical to suggest that with the advent of Victoria's death fashion

'An Edwardian lady in full dress was a wonder to behold, and her preparations for viewing were awesome'

William Manchester: 'The Last Lion'

styles changed overnight, but during the first few years of the new century a number of revolutionary changes took place which were to have a dramatic effect on the life style of fashionable society.

Under the rule of Victoria the Industrial Revolution had taken place, the British earning themselves a worldwide reputation for being disciplined industrialists and hard working, solid, dull, stern-faced pillars of society. The work ethic became master. When Edward came to the throne, however, he helped bring about the death of the strict and dour Victorian patriarchal society, abandoning solemnity in favour of gaiety and indulgence. For the court set and the wealthy it was play hard rather than work hard.

The court circle, together with the wealthy and the famous, controlled the high fashion of the period, but these influences quickly filtered down to the newly

Crowds on the river at Henley Regatta, July 1906

emergent middle class. Although fashionable court society still had its clothes made to measure by a couture house or a court dressmaker, similar less expensive, ready-to-wear versions of fashionable garment styles were now available in the new department stores and clothes shops. Improved printing methods enabled magazines to produce not only articles on fashion and style, but also home sewing and · knitting patterns. This meant that the wives of the new factory managers and their shop assistant daughters were not only better informed about the latest fashion look, but they could also reproduce watered-down copies of it by making clothes at home. Fashion was becoming more accessible than it had ever been.

A number of factors contribute to the development of a particular fashion look. These include prevailing economic and social conditions, technological and industrial change and developments in the arts and the media. Evidence of these influences is demonstrated in the garment style, design and detail, in the choice of fabric quality and colour, and in the shape of the body silhouette – perhaps the most important of these components.

In Edwardian times this was the famous 'S' shape. It came about as a result of the introduction of a new, supposedly healthier, corset. The medical profession was concerned that the Victorian corset was putting undue pressure on the rib cage. This very shapely garment had a curved metal busk down the front, which bowed out over the bust, curved in to a tiny waist and then curved out again to allow room for the stomach. When it was tightly laced to make the waist as tiny as possible it constricted the ribs.

To prevent this, the new healthy corset had a straight metal busk down the front, and did not emphasize the waist. Unfortunately Edwardian ladies liked their very tiny waists, so with great determination they pulled the laces of their new corsets very tight in an attempt to achieve the desired effect. The result, alas, was not the one they expected: the body was forced into a very odd, deformed shape instead.

The Edwardian Age in hit songs

1901	Just a-wearyin' for you
1902	Bill Bailey won't you please come home
1903	Sweet Adeline
1904	Give my regards to Broadway
1905	Wait till the sun shines, Nellie
1906	Waiting at the church
1907	If those lips could only speak
1908	Oh, oh Antonio
1909	I wonder who's kissing her now
1910	Ah! sweet mystery of life

The tighter the lacing was pulled, the more the top end of the new straight busk shot forward, while at the same time the bottom end of the busk pulled backwards. If one imagines a straight vertical line from the top of the head to the feet, in a side-on view, it is easy to visualize the bust forced forwards and down, and the hips pushed backwards and up. The resultant Edwardian 'S' shape has become a symbol of the era, providing an example of how technology and medicine can influence the fashion silhouette.

The elaborate lifestyle and exuberant ambience established by the extrovert Edward and his court set the mood for the rest of society and had a profound effect on fashion. He and his wife Alexandra had a keen interest in health and fitness, and they encouraged a wide range of leisure and sporting activities. These included tennis, golf, motoring, shooting, walking, riding and swimming, as well as attendance at parties, picnics, the theatre and race meetings. Very interested in good form, style and fashion, Edward was responsible for introducing into the court social circle a code of practice for correct dress for every occasion – and there were many occasions that required it.

Complying with a strict obligatory dress code for each of these activities meant a good many changes of clothes. An average day could require a morning outfit, a luncheon gown, a tea gown, dinner dress and theatre or formal evening dress, plus a special outfit for that round of golf or other sporting activity. Also to be worn were the essential accessories: parasols, rolled umbrellas, canes, walking sticks, gloves, fans, loads of jewellery, hats and hat-pins. Nobody, man, woman or child, ever went outdoors without a hat.

For both men and women, but particularly for women, this lifestyle and its rules and codes demanded a large wardrobe and a great deal of free time. Fashion may have been accessible to a wider public, but it still remained an expensive business.

When he came to the throne Edward was already fifty years old, and the friends of his court circle were of a similar age. He loved mature, confident, poised and beautiful women: to win his respect a woman was expected to be a good listener, knowledgeable, witty, charming, amusing, stylish and utterly feminine. Edward's vision of ideal womanhood was quickly adopted by society. Alexandra, his wife, epitomized this ideal: she was herself mature, poised and beautiful, and she set the style that others followed.

Edwardian high fashion was all about being elegant, tall and slender, and the illusion was created by the top-heavy look. Large hats with very wide brims and elaborate full-blown trimmings attracted the eye upwards. Abundant hair was worn off the face and piled on top of the head. High collars that were boned at the sides and sat tight to the neck made the face and neck look long and thin.

Wide sleeves, frills spreading over the shoulders or (for formal evenings) bare shoulders were all devices to attract the eye upwards and make the silhouette appear to be taller than it actually was. The lower half of the body, by contrast, was made to look very slender, the front of the full-length skirt being cut to fall slimly and smoothly over the hips, emphasizing the tiny waist and exaggerating length.

The back of the skirt was quite different: here there was always fullness. From the centre back waistline the fabric hung, sometimes over padding, in pleats and folds that ended either in a majestic train or in an elegant, bias-cut, swirling, fluted hem that trailed on the ground. When ladies walked, a mysterious and intriguing rustle of fabric accompanied them.

The Edwardian love of gaiety and indulgence was reflected in the choice of fabrics for ladies' wear. The fabrics were fine, frothy, floating and luxurious in quality and quantity. Silk, satin and georgette was exquisitely embroidered and decorated, especially when used for formal evening dresses, tea gowns and lingerie. The colours – fairy-like or sophisticated – might be sweet pea, sugar plum pastels or muted, intriguing shades of classic hues. The overall effect was light-hearted, confident, fun, flirty, but very grown up.

Theatrical, elaborate and romantic, this look was wonderfully exuberant and over the top but, amazingly, it all relied on that very peculiar deformed body shape. Fashion is ever evolving, however, and by 1907 the ultra elegant Edwardian style was being replaced by a new, modern, more natural look. The 'S' curve corset disappeared, and with it the elaborate lingerie, the fussy frills and the fairy-like colours and fabrics – never to return.

The attitude of women was also beginning to change. Better educated and able to get jobs, they were becoming more active and independent, their developing lifestyle requiring a less restrictive fashion. The new longer and straighter corset did not distort the figure, but produced a more natural straight up-and-down configuration to the silhouette, and a new fashion style evolved. By the time the king died in 1910 the High Edwardian fashion style that he had done so much to promote had also passed away.

Underneath it all

During the Edwardian era a new word was introduced into the English language: the garments that had previously been known as underwear were now called lingerie. The fact that this French word conjured up visions of romance and femininity was not a coincidence. It is true that lace trimmings and embroidery had been introduced by the Victorians and that the first silk underwear had appeared

'Edwardian underclothes developed a degree of eroticism never previously attempted. Women invented a silhouette of fictitious curves'

C. Willett & Phillis Cunnington: 'History of Underclothes'

in the 1880s, but Victorian undergarments remained functional, structured, stiff, drab and heavy. It was the Edwardian era that heralded revolutionary change.

In tune with the Edwardian 'Gay Nineties' mood, the fashionable way of life of the first decade of the twentieth century was lavish, and attendance at the sumptuous dinner parties, theatre visits, race meetings, and so on, demanded a plethora of elegant, glamorous clothes. It was generally considered that the elaborate outfits worn by the ladies should be worn only over equally glamorous and utterly feminine undergarments. Silk, satin, lace, ribbon, frills and flounces were the order of the day. Out went drab, stiff, serviceable and practical 'underwear',

Oo-la-la! Corsets in a late Edwardian window display, when long line models were replacing the Gibson Girl 'S' curve

and in came soft, flowing, light, airy, swishing and luxuriously feminine, romantic lingerie. Even the corset, which was of course the most important item in a lady's wardrobe, became lace-trimmed and alluring. The famous 'S' curve consisted of a lavish, bolster-shaped mono bosom, an incredibly tiny waist and backwards-sloping hips.

Under the corset it was usual to wear a chemise. Always trimmed with lace frills, this had a very low neck, was sleeveless and reached the knees. Under the chemise were what the Victorian had called drawers, but which were now known as knickers. These were still open: they had separate legs, often joined together only by the waistband. Occasionally the front had buttons part way down, leaving the crotch and centre back open. The legs, which were wide and reaching below the knee, ended with lots of frills, lace and ribbon.

Combining knickers with the chemise to create one garment was an innovation that became increasingly popular. The new combinations, as they were called, reduced bulk and allowed the bodice to fit even more tightly at the waist. Covering the corset was a camisole, which was like a lace-covered blouse drawn in at the waist. (The rows of lace could be stiffly starched, should extra help be needed to obtain the desired prominent bosom shape.)

Next came the petticoats – often more than one, the top one being called an underskirt. Petticoats and underskirts were shaped to follow the line of the figure: narrow and tight at the waist, fitted over the hip and thighs, and floating out to fullness below the knee. Edged with frills and lace, they were ankle-length at the front but long enough to sweep the floor at the back. When the wearer glided across the room, the petticoat frills were meant to be heard as well as be seen.

This new lingerie could now be purchased in matching sets and in a wide range of colours. The Frank Bentall catalogue advertised sets as being available in Old Rose, Amethyst, Emerald, Royal, Art Blue, Black stripe, Brown, Bronze and Grey-and-Whitestripe.

In view of this interest in colour it may seem strange that 95 per cent of the stockings purchased during the first decade of the twentieth century were black. Magazine articles of the period suggest that the smoke and dirt produced by the new industrials towns made it difficult to keep white and other pale colours clean, and black therefore became a more practical and popular alternative to socks and stockings.

Ladies and children wore black stockings for most occasions and for most activities (even swimming) and with most outfits, including white dresses. The general exception was when wearing formal evening gowns: on these occasions ladies often matched the colour of the stockings to that of the gown. These stockings were now mass-produced by powered circular machinery in large factories, leaving only the heel and toe to be joined by hand. There was a change in men's underwear, too: the new idea of combining garments saw the customary undervest and long pants transformed into 'combinations', knitted from pure natural wool.

Children's underwear imitated that of their parents. Even quite young girls wore a corset – not the restrictive, torturous garment that their mothers wore, but a boned and corded bodice band. In 1908 the liberty bodice was introduced, and for the next thirty years or so this soft-knitted article became normal wear for girls. Like their mothers, girls also wore lace- and ribbon-trimmed petticoats and knickers, these reaching to just beneath the knee for children, and to mid-calf for the older girl. The lace was meant to show below their dresses.

The patterns on the next few pages are intended to illustrate something of the mood and flavour of the Edwardian era. The decision to use white yarn for most of the undies was more to do with my personal preference than any attempt at authenticity. In fact, had the originals been white they certainly would not have been the bright blue-white that modern chemical dyes allow. A dirty looking off-white colour would be more correct, but the choice is yours – and if you are really intent on realism, no one is insisting that you stitch up that crotch seam!

LADY'S UNDERSKIRT AND MATCHING KNICKERS

This simple underskirt will fit under a day dress or a simple skirt. The back hem is very slightly shaped by knitting short rows. (Check the Knitting Methods on page 4 for instructions on how to work neat hole-less short rows). In order to avoid having a centre front seam, the knickers are knitted in one piece.

Materials
- A pair each of size 22, and size 20 needles
- 100m reel of Gütermann pure silk, S303, in white (col 800)

Tension
9sts and 11 rows equal 1cm (⅜in), using size 20 needles over st st

Abbreviations
sl2tog-k1-p2sso: place the point of the right hand needle into the next 2sts as if to k2tog, but instead, slip them both onto the right hand needle, k the next st, then pass the 2 slipped sts over and off the needle.

LACE PATTERN
1st row: k1, *k1, yfwd, k3, sl2tog-k1-p2sso, k3, yfwd,* rep from * to last 2sts k2,
2nd row, and all alt rows: p to end
3rd row: k3, *yfwd, k2, sl2tog-k1-p2sso, k2, yfwd, k3* rep from * to end,
5th row: k1, k2tog, *yfwd, k1, yfwd, k1, sl2tog-k1-p2sso, k1, yfwd, k1, yfwd, sl2tog-k1-p2sso,
6th row: p
These 6 rows form the patt and are repeated.

UNDERSKIRT
FRONT
**Using size 22 needles cast on 143 sts and p 1 row, then work 3 reps of the lace patt
Next row: k1, [k2tog] to end (72sts)
Next 3 rows: p
Work insertion holes

4cm
(1⅝in)

Front

Back

9cm
(3½in)

Next row: k2, [yfwd, k2tog], to end,
Next 3 rows: p,
Change to size 20 needles**
Beg With a k row, work 2 rows in st st
***Shape sides
Cont in st st and dec 1 st. at each end of the 7th row, then each end of the [foll 10th row] twice, the [foll 6th row] twice, the [foll 4th row] 5 times, then the foll 8 alt rows. Finish with a wrong side row, (36sts)
Cast off. ***

BACK

Work from ** to ** to match the front
Shape hem
Next row: k57, turn,
Next row: sl1, p39, turn,
Next row: sl1, k34, turn,
Next row: sl1, p29, turn,
Next row: sl1, k24, turn,
Next row: sl1, p19, turn,
Next row: sl1, k14, turn,
Next row: sl1, p9, turn,
Next row: sl1, k to end,
Next row: p
Cont now to work from *** to *** to match the front.

KNICKERS

Work the first leg
**Using size 22 needles, cast on 103 sts and p1 row.
Now work 2 reps of the lace patt
Next row: k1, [k2tog] to end,. (52 sts)
Next 3 rows: p,
Next row: k2, [yfwd, k2tog] to end
Next 3 rows: p
Change to size 20 needles,

Shape leg
Working in st st beg with a k row and inc 1 st. at each end of the foll 5th row, then each end of the [foll 6th row] twice, the [foll 4th row] twice, then the [foll alt row] 4 times. Finish with a WS row. (70 sts)
Shape crotch seam
Cast off 3 sts at the beg of the next 4 rows, then dec 1 st. at each end of the next row, and the foll 2 alt rows, finish with a p row. (52 sts)**
Leave these sts on a spare needle.
Work the second leg
Foll patt for first leg from** to **
Join the legs
Knit the next row of the second leg, then making sure that you have the right side facing, knit the sts from the spare needle. (104 sts)
Cont in st st for 21 rows,
Cast off.

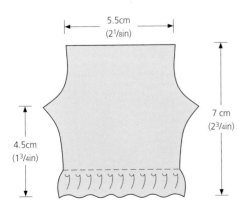

5.5cm
(2¹/₈in)

7 cm
(2³/₄in)

4.5cm
(1³/₄in)

TO MAKE UP

Bag out, block and steam the knitted pieces, following the instructions in the section on finishing (page 6).

Underskirt. Join the side seams, and thread ribbon or stranded cotton through the insertion holes at the hem. Decorate with bows as preferred. Run a gathering thread round the waistline, and pull up to fit, adjust the gathers so that most of the fullness is at the back.

Knickers. Join the inside leg seam on each leg, then stitch the centre back seam and the back and front crotch seams. Thread ribbon or stranded cotton through the insertion holes at hem. Run a gathering thread round the waistline, and draw up to fit.

A PARTY PETTICOAT

This lady's half-slip has a shaped train with fullness at the centre back and lots of lace trim. Very pretty, it will also give added shape to glamorous tea and evening gowns. It can be worn with the matching camisole and knickers.

The slip is knitted in four panels: one front panel, two sides and a back panel. The hem is shaped with short rows.

Materials
- A pair of size 20 needles,
- Two 100m reels of Gütermann pure silk, S303 in white (col 800)
- Narrow silk ribbon for decoration.

Tension
9sts and 11 rows equal 1 cm (⅜in), using size 20 needles over st st

Abbreviations
sl2tog-k1-p2sso: place the point of the right hand needle into the next 2 sts as if to k2tog but do not work them, instead slip them both onto the right hand needle, k the next st, then pass the 2 slipped sts over this st. and off the needle. ssk [slip 1 st knitwise], twice, then approaching from the left, insert the point of the LH needle into the front of these 2sts, and knit them tog from this position.

LACE PATTERN 'A'
1st row: p1, ssk, [yfwd, k1] 3 times, yfwd, k2tog, p1,
2nd row: k1, p9, k1,
3rd row: p1, ssk, k5, k2tog, p1,
4th row: k1, p7, k1,
These 4 rows form the pattern and are repeated.

LACE EDGING
Cast on 11 sts and k 1 row,
1st row: k3, yfwd, k2tog, k1, ssk, turn, cast on 4sts, turn, k2tog, k1, (13sts)
2nd row: k10, yfwd, k2tog, turn,
3rd row: k2, yfwd, k2tog, ssk, [yfwd, k1] 4 times, yfwd, k2tog,
4th row: k13, yfwd, k2tog, k1,
5th row: k3, yfwd, k2tog, ssk, [yfwd, k1] twice, yfwd, sl1-k2tog-psso, [yfwd, k1] twice, yfwd, k2tog,

6th row: k15, yfwd; k2tog, turn,
7th row: k2, yfwd, k2tog, k11, k2tog,
8th row: cast off 6sts, k7, yo, k2tog, k1, (11sts)
These 8 rows form the patt and are repeated.

FRONT PANEL

Using size 20 needles, cast on 37sts, and p 1 row,
Work insertion holes
Next row: [k2tog, yfwd], rep to last st, k1,
Next 3 rows: p,
Next row: [k2tog, yfwd], rep. to last st, k1,
Next row: (WS), k,
Shape sides
Next row: k2tog, k12, [row 1, patt A], k12, k2tog,
Next row: p13, [row 2, patt A], p13,
Next row: k13, [row 3, patt A], k13,
Next row: p13, [row 4, patt A], p13,
Work the lace patt as now set, **but at the same time,** dec 1 st, at each end of the foll 4th row, then each end of the [foll 8th row] 5 times, [each foll 4th row] 4 times, and [each foll 2nd row] 3 times. Patt 2 rows,
Cast off rem 9sts

RIGHT SIDE PANEL

* Using size 20 needles cast on 58sts, and p 1 row,
Work insertion holes
Next row: [k2tog, yfwd], to last 2 sts, k2
Next 3 rows: p,
Next row: [k2tog, yfwd], to last 2 sts, k2,
Next row: (WS), k*
Shape hem by working short rows as follows.
Next row: k52, turn,
Next row: sl1, p43, turn,
Next row: sl1, k to end,
Next row: p2tog, p40, turn,
Next row: sl1, k to last 2 sts, k2tog,
Next row: p2tog, p30, turn,
Next row: sl1, k to last 2 sts, k2tog,
Next row: p2tog, p20, turn,
Next row: sl1, k to last 2 sts, k2tog,
Next row: p2tog, p10, turn,
Next row: sl1, k to last 2 sts, k2tog,
Next row: p to end, (50 sts)
Shape side
Working in st st, beg with a k row, and dec 1 st. at the end of every k row until there are 27 sts.
Then dec 1 st. at the same edge of [each foll 4th row], 5 times, then work 3 rows straight. (22sts)

Shape hip dart:
1st row: k8, sl2tog-k1-p2sso, k to last 2 sts, k2tog
2nd, 4th, 6th, 8th rows: p
3rd row: k to last 2sts, k2tog,
5th row: k7, sl2tog-k1-p2sso, k to last 2 sts k2tog,
7th row: as 3rd row
9th row: k6, sl2tog-k1-p2sso, k to last 2 sts, k2tog (11 sts)
10th row: p5, turn,
11th row: sl1, k4,
12th row: p,
13th row: cast off.

LEFT SIDE PANEL

Work from * to* as RH panel, then k 1 row, to finish with WS facing,
Shape hem by working short rows as folls.
Next row: p52, turn,
Next row: sl1, k43, turn,
Next row: sl1, p to end,
Next row: k2tog, k40, turn,
Next row: sl1, p to last 2 sts, p2tog,
Next row: k2tog, k30, turn,
Next row: sl1, p to last 2 sts p2tog,
Next row: k2tog, k20, turn,
Next row: sl1, p to last 2 sts, p2tog,
Next row: k2tog, k10, turn,
Next row: sl1, p to last 2 sts, p2tog,
Shape side
Working in st st right across the rows, beg with a k row, and dec 1 st. at the beg of every k row until there are 27 sts.
Then dec 1 st. at the same edge of [each foll 4th row], 5 times; then work 3 rows straight. (22sts)

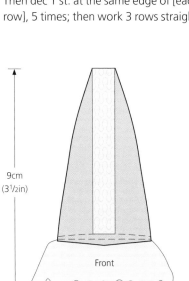

Front

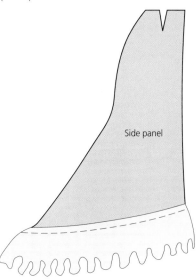

Side panel

9cm
(3½in)

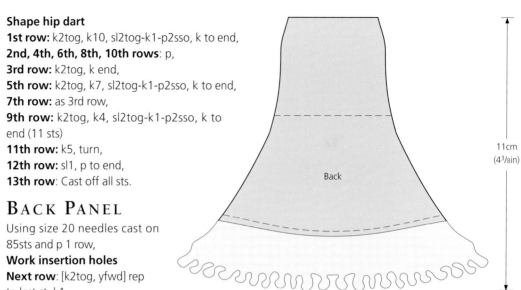

11cm
(4³/₈in)

Back

Shape hip dart

1st row: k2tog, k10, sl2tog-k1-p2sso, k to end,
2nd, 4th, 6th, 8th, 10th rows: p,
3rd row: k2tog, k end,
5th row: k2tog, k7, sl2tog-k1-p2sso, k to end,
7th row: as 3rd row,
9th row: k2tog, k4, sl2tog-k1-p2sso, k to end (11 sts)
11th row: k5, turn,
12th row: sl1, p to end,
13th row: Cast off all sts.

BACK PANEL

Using size 20 needles cast on 85sts and p 1 row,
Work insertion holes
Next row: [k2tog, yfwd] rep to last st. k1,
Next 3 rows: p,
Next row: [k2tog, yfwd], rep to last st, k1,
Next row: (WS), k,
Shape centre of panel
Beg with a k row, and work 6 rows st st
Next row: k1, ssk, k21, ssk, k33, k2tog, k21, k2tog, k1,
Work 5 rows st st
Next row: k1, ssk, k20, ssk, k31, k2tog, k20, k2tog, k1,
work 5 rows st st
Next row: k1, ssk, k19, ssk, k29, k2tog, k19, k2tog, k1,

Work 5 rows st st
Next row: k1, ssk, k18, ssk, k27, k2tog, k18, k2tog, k1,
Work 5 rows st st
Next row: k1, ssk, k17, ssk, k25, k2tog, k17, k2tog, k1,
Work 5 rows st. st.
Next row: k1, ssk, k16, ssk, k23, k2tog, k16, k2tog, k1,
Work 5 rows st st
Next row: k1, ssk, k15, ssk, k21, k2tog, k15, k2tog, k1,
Work 5 rows st st
Next row: k1, ssk, k14, ssk, k19, k2tog, k14, k2tog, k1,
Work 5 rows st. st.
Next row: k1, ssk, k13, ssk, k17, k2tog, k13, k2tog, k1,
Next row: p,
Work gathering row
Next row: [k1, k2tog, yo], rep. to last st, k1.
Work 3 rows st st
Cont in st st but now dec 1 st at each end of the next row, and then [every foll 6th row], 5 times, [every foll 4th row], 4 times, (29sts),
Work 3 rows straight, then cast off.

HEM EDGING

Using size 20 needles, cast on 11 sts, and work the lace-edging patt. To reach all round the hem, you should need to knit 60 reps of the patt or 30cms in length, but measure the edging round the hem before casting off.

TO MAKE UP

Bag out, block and steam the knitted pieces, following the instructions in the section on finishing (page 6).

Stitch the straight edges of the side panels to the centre-front panel, then stitch the back panel into place leaving about 2cm (¾in) open at the waist end of one seam. With RS together, over-sew the lace edging to the hem

Thread very narrow ribbon or stranded cotton through the insertion eyelet holes at the hem, and decorate with bows as appropriate.

Run a gathering thread through the holes at centre back knee level and pull up to measure 1.5cm (⅝in).

Fit the petticoat to your doll and finish stitching up the incomplete seam, gather up centre back waist to fit.

CAMISOLE AND MATCHING KNICKERS

This little camisole top also matches the party petticoat. It would be unusual for a doll to wear this sort of garment under a top garment as it creates too much bulk, but the camisole could be useful if the doll is to be displayed wearing only her underwear.

Materials
- A pair of size 20 needles
- 50m reel of Gütermann pure silk S303 in white (col 800)

Tension
9sts and 11 rows equal 1 cm (⅜in), using size 20 needles over st st

Abbreviations
ssk, [slip 1 st knitwise] twice, then approaching from the left, insert the point of the LH needle into the front of these 2sts, and knit them tog from this position.
Sl2tog-k1-p2sso, place the point of the RH needle into the next 2sts as if to k2tog, but do not work them, instead slip them both onto the RH needle, k the next st., then pass the 2 slipped sts over the knitted st. and off the needle.

LACE PATTERN 'A'
1st row: p1, ssk, [yfwd, k1] 3 times, yfwd, k2tog, p1, ssk, [yfwd, k1] 3 times, yfwd, k2tog, p1,
2nd row: k1, p19, k1,
3rd row: p1, ssk, k5, k2tog, p1, ssk, k5, k2tog, p1,
4th row: k1, p15, k1,

ARMHOLE LACE EDGING
Using size 20 needles, cast on 4 sts, p1 row,
1st row: k1, p3,
2nd row: k1, yfwd, k1 tbl, yfwd, sl1-k1-psso,
3rd row: k1, p2, [k1, p1, k1, p1] into next st., p1,
4th Row: cast off 4 sts, k1, yfwd, sl1-k1-psso,
These 4 rows form the patt and are repeated for the required length.

KNICKER LACE EDGING
Cast on 11 sts and k 1 row,

1st row: k3, yfwd, k2tog, k1, ssk, turn, cast on 4sts, turn, k2tog, k1, (13sts)
2nd row: k10, yfwd, k2tog, turn,
3rd row: k2, yfwd, k2tog, ssk, [yfwd, k1] 4 times, yfwd, k2tog,
4th row: k13, yfwd, k2tog, k1,
5th row: k3, yfwd, k2tog, ssk, [yfwd, k1] twice, yfwd, sl1-k2tog-psso, [yfwd, k1] twice, yfwd, k2tog,
6th row: k15, yfwd, k2tog, turn,
7th row: k2, yfwd, k2tog, k11, k2tog,
8th row: cast off 6sts, k7, yo, k2tog, k1, (11sts)
These 8 rows form the patt and are repeated.

CAMISOLE

FRONT
**Using size 20 needles, cast on 47sts, and k 2 rows,
Next row: k2tog, k to last 2 sts, k2tog,
Next row: p,
Next row: k2tog, k9, sl2tog-k1-p2sso, k17, sl2tog-k1-p2sso, k9, k2tog,
Next row: p,
Next row: k2tog, k7, sl2tog-k1-p2sso, k15, sl2tog-k1-p2sso, k7, k2tog,
Next row: p, (33sts)

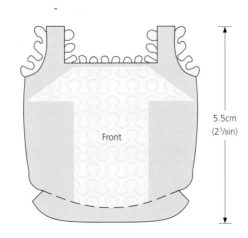

Front

5.5cm (2⅛in)

Work waist insertion holes

Next row: [k2tog, yfwd] rep to last st, k1

Next row: p**

Next row: k5 [k twice into next st] 24 times, k4 (57sts)

Next row: p to end,

Shape bodice

1st row: k20, (row 1, lace patt 'A'), k2tog, turn,

2nd row: sl1, (row 2, lace patt 'A'), p2tog, turn,

3rd row: sl1, (row 3, lace patt 'A'), k2tog, k3, turn,

4th row: sl1, p3, (row 4, lace patt 'A'), p2tog, p3, turn,

5th row: sl1, k3, (row 1, lace patt 'A'), k3, k2tog, k3, turn

6th row: sl1, p6, (row 2, lace patt 'A'), p3, p2tog, p3, turn,

7th row: sl1, k6, (row 3, lace patt 'A'), k6, k2tog, k3, turn,

8th row: sl1, p9, (row 4, lace patt 'A'), p6, p2tog, p3, turn,

9th row: sl1, k9, [row 1, lace patt 'A'], k9, k2tog, k3, turn,

10th row: sl1, p12, [row 2, lace patt 'A'], p9, p2tog, p3, turn,

11th row: sl1, k12, [row 3, lace patt 'A'], k9, k2tog, k4,

12th row: p14, [row 4, lace patt 'A'], p9, p2tog, p4, (45sts)

Working the central patt as set, cont without shaping, until 5 more reps of the lace patt have been worked.

Next row: k6, p1, ssk, [yfwd, k1] 3 times, yfwd, k2tog, [row 1, lace patt 'A'], ssk, [yfwd, k1] 3 times, yfwd, k2tog, p1, k6,

Next row: p

Next row: k6, p1, ssk, k5, k2tog, [row 3, lace patt 'A'], ssk, k5, k2tog, p1, k6,

Next row: p,

rep. the last 4 rows once more.

Shape armholes and neck

Work the central lace panel as now set, and cast off 2sts at the beg of the next 4 rows,

Next row: cast off 2 sts, k7, cast off 17sts, k to end,

Next row: cast off 2sts, p7, turn, k8,

Next row: cast off 2sts, p5, turn, k6,

Working on these 6sts only, work 6 more rows in st st

Cast off.

With WS facing return to the rem sts, rejoin yarn and p to end,

Cast off 2sts at beg of next row, then work

straight for 7 more rows,
Cast off.

BACK

Work from ** to **, to match the front,

Beg with a k row, work in st st and inc 1 st. at each end of the 3rd row, then [each foll 4th row] 5 times, (45sts)

Work 5 rows st st

Shape armholes

Cast of 2sts at the beg of the next 4 rows,

Next row: cast off 2 sts, k7, cast off 17sts, k to end,

Next row: cast off 2sts p7, turn, k8,

Next row: cast off 2sts, p5, turn, cont on these 6sts only, and work 7 rows st st. Cast off.

With WS facing rejoin yarn to rem sts, p to end,

Cast off 2sts at the beg of next row, work 7 more rows in st st. Cast off.

EDGE TRIMS

Armhole lace

Work 2 lengths of 10 reps of the armhole lace edging.

Neck edging

Work 11 reps of the armhole lace edging.

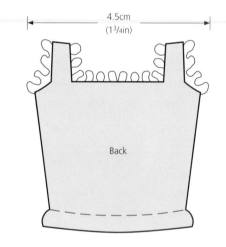

4.5cm
(1³/₄in)

Back

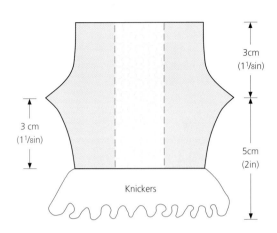

Knickers

KNICKERS

Using size 20 needles, cast on 53sts, and p1 row,
Work insertion holes
Next row: [k2tog, yfwd] rep to last st, k1,
Next 3 rows: p,
Next row: [k2tog, yfwd,] rep to last st, k1,
Next row: (WS), k
Shape leg
Next row: k18, [row 1, lace patt A], k18,
Next row: p18, [row 2, lace patt A] p18,
Next row: k18, [row 3, lace patt A], k18,
Next row: p18, [row 4, lace patt A], p18,
Working in patt as now set, inc 1 st at each end
of the next row, then each end of the [foll 4th
row] 4 times, [the foll alt row] 4 times, finish with
a WS row, (71sts)
Shape crotch seam
Keeping the lace patt correct, cast off 3 sts at the
beg of the next 4 rows, then dec 1 st at each end
of the next row, and the foll 2 alt rows, finish
with a WS row, (53sts)
Leave these sts on a spare needle.
Work a second leg to match,
Join legs
Patt the next row of the second leg, then making
sure that you have the RS facing, patt across the
sts from spare needle. (106sts)
Keeping the patt correct, work 19 more rows,
Cast off.

LACE EDGING

Using size 20 needles, cast on 11 sts, work 12
repeats of the knicker edging patt then measure
the lace against the knicker leg before casting off.

TO MAKE UP

Bag out, block and steam the pieces following the
instructions in the section on finishing (page 6).

Camisole. Join shoulder seams. With RS together
over-sew the lace trim to the armhole edges. Join
the ends of the neck-lace, and with RS together
over-sew into place round the neck edge. Carefully
steam the neck and armhole edges, then gently
persuade the lace into place, so that the points lie
towards the wearer's face on the neckline. The
armhole lace should look like short sleeves.

Join the side seams.

Add a small bow to centre front neck and one to
centre-front waist. Fit to doll and run a gathering
thread or ribbon through the insertion holes, and
draw up to fit.

Knickers. Join each leg seam, then stitch the
crotch seam. With right sides facing over-sew the
lace edging to each leg. Thread ribbon or stranded
cotton through the insertion holes, decorate with
bows as preferred.

Run a gathering thread round the waistline and
draw up to fit.

Child's Underskirt and Knickers To fit a 10cm (4 inch) Doll

Materials
- A pair of size 20 needles
- 100m reel of Gütermann pure silk S303 in white (col 800)

Tension
9sts and 11 rows equal 1cm (⅜in), using size 20 needles, over st st

Abbreviations
ssk, [slip 1 st knitwise] twice, then, approaching from the left, insert the point of the LH needle into the front of these 2sts, and knit them tog from this position.
sl2tog-k1-p2sso, place the point of the RH needle into the next 2 sts as if to k2tog, do not work them, but instead, slip them both onto the RH needle, k the next st., then pass the 2 slipped sts, over the knitted st. and off the needle

LACE EDGING PATTERN
Using size 20 needles, cast on 4 sts and k 1 row,
1st row: k2, yfwd, k2
2nd row: k2, yfwd, k1, yfwd, k2,
3rd row: k2, yfwd, k3, yfwd, k2,
4th row: k2, yfwd, k5, yfwd, k2,
5th row: k2, yfwd, ssk, k3, k2tog, yfwd, k2,
6th row: k3, yfwd, ssk, k1, k2tog, yfwd, k3,
7th row: k4, yfwd, sl1-k2tog-psso, yfwd, k4,
8th row: cast off 7sts, k3. (4sts)
These 8 rows form the patt and are repeated.

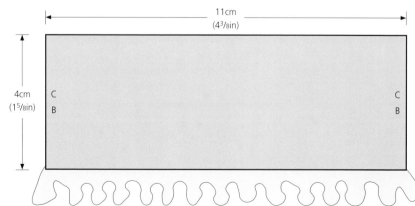

11cm
(4³/₈in)

4cm
(1⁵/₈in)

C
B

C
B

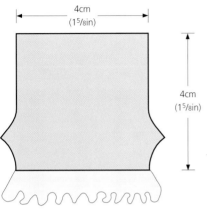

4cm
(1⁵/₈in)

4cm
(1⁵/₈in)

UNDERSKIRT

Using size 20 needles, cast on 100sts, and p 1 row,
Work insertion holes
Next row: [p2tog, yrn], to last 2 sts, k2
Next 2 rows: p,
Beg with a k row, work 40 rows in st st, Cast off.

LACE EDGING

You will need 20 reps of the lace patt

KNICKERS

** Using size 20 needles cast on 40sts, and p 1 row,
Next row: [p2tog, yrn] to last 2 sts, p2,
Next 2 rows: p
Shape crotch
Beg with a k row, work in st st and inc 1 st. at each end of the next 5 rows, then p 1 row,
Dec 1 st. at each end of the next 5 rows,**
Leave these sts on a spare needle, and work a second leg to match.
Join legs
Make sure that you have the RS of both legs facing you, knit across the sts of the second leg, then cont across the sts on the spare needle, (80sts),
Cont in st st for 17 more rows. Cast off.

LACE EDGING

For each leg you will need 8 reps of the lace patt.

TO MAKE UP

Bag out, block and steam the pieces following the instructions in the section on finishing (page 6).

Underskirt. Overcase the lace edging to the cast-on edge of the skirt, then join the centre-back seam. Run a gathering thread through the waistline, pull up to fit.

Knickers. With right sides together, over-sew a length of lace trim to the cast-on edge of each leg. Join each leg seam. Join centre-back seam and back then front crotch seam. Thread ribbon or stranded cotton through the insertion holes and decorate with bows.

MAN'S COMBINATIONS

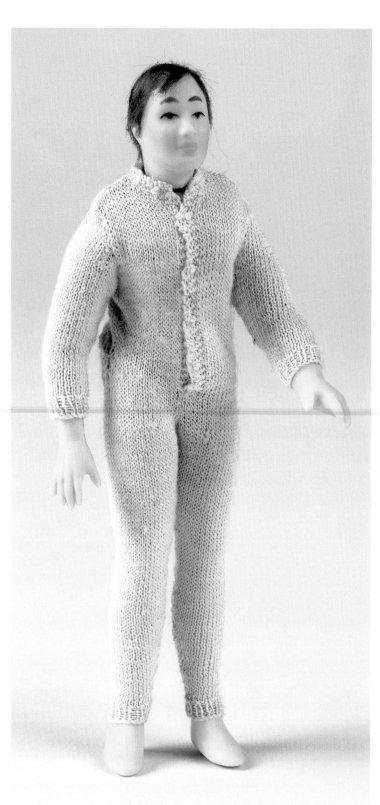

The main body of this garment is knitted in one piece. At the centre back there is a buttoned flap, which is knitted when the rest of the body is finished. When this point is reached it might be easier to leave the 'flap' stitches on a length of waste thread, rather than a spare needle.

Materials
- A pair each of size 20 and size 21 needles
- 100m reel of Gütermann pure silk S303 in cream (col 802)

Tension
9sts and 11 rows equal 1cm (⅜in), using size 20 needles over st st

Abbreviations
ssk, [slip 1 st knitwise] twice, then approaching from the left, insert the point of the LH needle into the front of these 2sts, then knit them tog from this position.
m1, make 1 stitch, pick up the thread that is stretched between the needles, and knit into the back loop of it.

MAIN BODY
Work legs
Using size 21 needles, cast on 24 sts, work 6 rows in k1, p1, rib,
Change to size 20 needles,
Beg with a k row, work in st st and inc 1 st at each end of the 5th row, then [every foll 6th row] 10 times, [each foll alt row] 5 times, finish with a WS row. (56sts),
Cast off 3sts, at beg of next 2 rows, and 2sts at beg of foll 2 rows. Now dec 1 st at each end of the next row, and the foll 2 alt rows. (40sts).
Finish with a p row then leave sts on a spare needle.
Work a second leg to match.
Join legs
k the next row of second leg, then making sure that the RS is facing, cont to k across the sts from the first leg, (80sts)
Beg with a p row, work 5 rows in st st
Work back opening
Next row: cast on 2 sts, k the 2sts, plus the next 20. Place the next 40sts onto a spare needle,

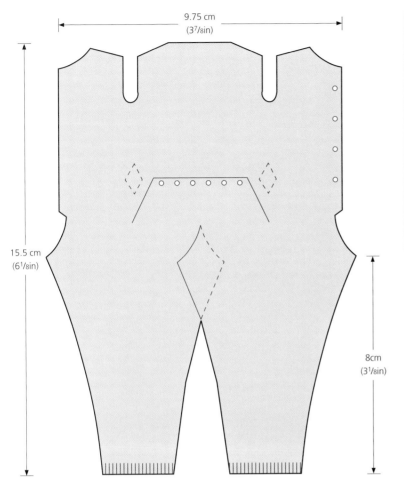

9.75 cm
(3⁷/₈in)

15.5 cm
(6¹/₈in)

8cm
(3¹/₈in)

turn, cast on 40 sts, turn back again and cont to k across the rem sts on LH needle (82sts)

Next row: cast on 2 sts, k4, p to last 4 sts, k4,

Next row: k20, ssk, k40, k2tog, k20,

Next row: K4, p to last 4 sts, k4,

Next row: k19, ssk, k40, k2tog, k16, yfwd, k2tog, k1

Next row: k4, p to last 4 sts k4,

Next row: k18, ssk, [k4, k2tog] 7 times, k18, (72sts)

Next row: k4, p to last 4sts, k4

Next row: k to end,

Next row: k4, p to last 4sts, k4,

Shape chest section

1st row: k18, m1, k2, m1, k32, m1, k2, m1, k15, yfwd, k2tog, k1,

2nd and all alt rows: k4, p to last 4 sts, k4,

3rd row: k,

5th row: k19, m1, k2, m1, k34, m1, k2, m1, k to end,

7th row: k to end

9th row: k20, m1, k2, m1, k36, m1, k2, m1, k to end,

11th row: k,

13th row: k21, m1, k2, m1, k38, m1, k2, m1, k to last 3 sts, yfwd, k2tog, k1,

14th row: k4, p to last 4sts, p4

Cont in st st without shaping for 8 more rows

Divide for armholes

Next row: k21, cast off 4sts, k37, cast off 4sts, k to end

Next row: k4, p17, turn, cont on these sts only

to complete the left front,

Next row: k2tog, k to last 3sts, yfwd, k2tog, k1,

Next row: k4, p16,

Keeping edge sts correct, work 10 rows without shaping,

Next row: k17, yfwd, k2tog, k1,

Work 8 rows straight to finish at neck edge,

Shape neck

Cast off 7sts at beg of next row, then, patt to end,

Cast off 5 sts at the beg of the next row, 3sts at beg of foll row, then cast off rem 5sts

Work back armholes

With WS facing, rejoin yarn to sts on LH needle, p38, turn,

Cont on these sts only and dec 1st at each end of the next row then work 21 rows without shaping

Cast off 5sts at the beg of the next 4 rows, then cast off rem 16sts.

Work right front

With WS facing rejoin yarn to rem sts, p to last 4sts, k4,

Next row: k to last 2sts, k2tog,

Keeping the edge sts of button band in g st, work 21 rows straight,

Cast off 7sts at the neck edge of the next row, 5sts at the beg of the next row, 3sts at beg of foll row, then cast off rem 5sts,

Work back flap

With RS facing return to the centre back opening sts, rejoin yarn,

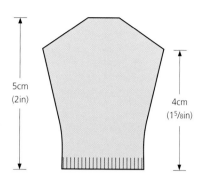

5cm (2in)

4cm (1⁵/₈in)

Next row: k to end,

Next row: k3, p to last 3 sts, k3,

Next row: k35, turn,

Next row: sl1, p29, turn,

Next row: sl1, k24, turn,

Next row: sl1, p19, turn,

Next row: sl1, k14, turn,

Next row: sl1, p9,

Next row: sl1, k to end,

Now work 16 rows, without shaping across all of the sts

Next row: k3, p1, [p2tog, p3] to last 6sts, p2tog, p1, k3, (33sts)

Change to size 21 needles,

Work 2 rows, in st st

Next row: k3, [yfwd, k2tog, k3] 5 times, yfwd, k2tog, k3,

k 2 rows, then cast off knit-wise.

SLEEVES

Using size 21 needles, cast on 24sts, work in k1, p1, rib for 6 rows,

Change to size 20 needles, work in st st and shape the sides as folls.

Inc 1 st at each end of the next row, and each foll 6th row, until there are 36sts,

Work 7 rows straight,

Shape top

Cast off 2sts at the beg of the next 4 rows, then dec 1 st at each end of the next row and the foll 3 alt rows, then dec 1st at each end of the next 5 rows, cast off rem 10sts.

Work a second sleeve to match.

NECK BAND

Using size 21 needles, cast on 44sts, then cast them off.

TO MAKE UP

Bag out, block and steam the pieces following the instructions in the section on finishing (page 6).

Join the shoulder seams.

To sew on the neck-band, place the neck band cast-on stitches to the neckline. Start at the outside corner of L front, stitch together for 2sts, then miss 2sts to make a small buttonhole. Cont to stitch the band into place finishing at the outside corner of the R front. Use steam to ensure that the band stands up slightly with the cast-off edge towards the face.

Stitch each leg seam, then join the crotch seam. Join the sleeve seams, and stitch the sleeves into place.

Over-lap the centre-front bands left over right and secure the ends, stitch on buttons to match the button holes.

SOCKS AND STOCKINGS

These long stockings and the knee-high socks are knitted on two needles, with a centre back seam. Knitting begins at the toe and finishes with a narrow ribbed top. Instructions for the stockings are given in two sizes, the smaller size will fit a 10cm (4 inch) child doll, the larger size (enclosed in round brackets), will fit a 14cm (5½ inch) lady doll. The socks will fit a 10cm, (4inch) child doll.

Materials
- A pair of size 20 and size 21 needles,
- 50m reel of Gütermann pure silk S303 in black (col 000)

Tension
10sts and 13 rows equal 1cm (⅜in), using size 21 needles over st st

Abbreviations
m1: make one stitch, pick up the loop lying between the stitches of the previous row and place on LH needle, then knit it through the back loop.

STOCKINGS
Using size 21 needles cast on 19 (25) sts, and work 4 (6) rows in st st
Shape toe
Next row: k1, m1, k8 (11), m1, k1, m1, k8 (11), m1, k1,
Next row: p
Next row: k2, m1, k8 (11), m1, k3, m1, k8 (11), m1, k2,
Next row: p

LARGER SIZE ONLY
Next row: k3, m1, k11, m1, k5, m1, k11, m1, k3,
Next row: p, (27 (37), sts)

BOTH SIZES
Shape foot
Next row: k14 (21), k2tog, turn,
Next row: sl1, p3 (p5), p2tog, turn,
Next row: sl1, k3 (k5), k2tog, turn,
Next row: sl1, p3 (p5), p2tog, turn,
Rep the last 2 rows until there are a total of 15 (23) sts, counting right across the row, then sl1 and k to end,

Beg with a p row and work 5 (7) rows in st st
Shape leg
inc 1 st. at each end of the next row, and the 4 (5) foll alt rows,
Work 5 (7) rows straight,
Dec 1 st at each end of the next row, and [foll 3rd (4th) row] twice, (19 (29) sts)
Now [inc 1 st. at each end of the foll 4th row] 3 (4) times, (25 (37) sts)
Work 3 rows in st st then 4 rows in single rib (k1, p1),
Cast off very loosely using a size 19 needles.

BOY'S KNEE LENGTH SOCKS
Using size 20 needles cast on 20sts, and work 4 rows in st st
Shape toe
Next row: k1, m1, k8, m1, k2, m1, k8, m1, k1,
Next row: p
Next row: k2, m1, k8, m1, k4, m1, k8, m1, k2,
Next row: p (28sts)
Next row: k16, k2tog, turn,
Next row: sl1, p4, p2tog, turn,
Next row: sl1, k4, k2tog, turn,
Next row: sl1, p4, p2tog, turn,
Rep the last 2 rows until there are a total of 16sts, counting all sts, then sl1 and k to end of row,
Next row: [k1, p1], to end,
Cont now in rib as set, and work 4 rows straight,
Shape leg
Keeping rib correct, inc 1 st. at each end of the next row, then each end of the [foll 4th row] twice,
Work 5 rows straight,
Dec 1 st at each end of the next row and the foll 4th row,
Work 3 rows in rib, then using a larger size needle, cast off in rib.

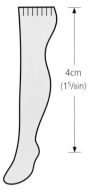

Girl's stocking

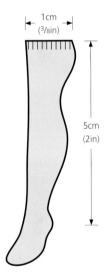

Lady's stocking

TO MAKE UP

Bag out, block and steam the pieces following the instructions in the section on finishing (page 6).

With right sides together join each leg and foot seam. Turn through to the right side.

A morning at home

Edwardian ladies wore blouses and skirts for everyday wear around the home. Always worn over a very rigid structure, the blouses fell in soft folds over the bust, with elaborate trimmings such as lace, beading, embroidery or fringing and a very high neck. The long sleeves were a simpler

'No great lady ever wears out a dress. She appears in a charming outfit a few times, until all her social set have admired it, and then she disposes of it to private agents who sell it again or export it to the Colonies'

Berrow's Worcester Journal, August 1901

version of the Victorian leg-of-mutton sleeve, very full and wide at the top, narrow and tapering over the elbow and lower arm. The fabrics used were soft, delicate and feminine, with lots of ribbon, lace and bows.

The full-length tailored skirts were fluted to skim the hips, and they became wider at the hem, sweeping outwards with a short train at the back. They often had fullness at

Home entertainment, 1908

the centre-back in the form of soft unpressed pleats, and were worn over a petticoat that also had extra fabric at the centre back, giving the effect of a slightly padded rear. The 'must have' tiny waist was often emphasised with a wide belt. Small bags for hankies, loose change or keys were sometimes suspended from the waist belt.

Men wore a lounge suit for mornings at home and, with the addition of a bowler or Homburg hat, for everyday town wear. The three-piece suit, made from a tweed or woollen fabric, had a short single-breasted jacket with straight sleeves, straight-leg trousers and a matching single-breasted waistcoat. The shirt usually had a winged collar and was worn with a long narrow, knotted tie.

Day wear for small children from six months up to three or four years old – both girls and boys – was a dress which reached just below the knee. At about four years old the boys had their hair cut and were now allowed to wear short trousers with blouses or little jackets. As they got older they wore suits. The sailor suit and the Norfolk suit – a wool or tweed jacket worn with knickerbockers – were particularly popular. The Norfolk jacket had a long pleat down each front, centre buttons and a belt. The knickerbockers came to the knee and were rather fuller than breeches. The suit was worn with a cap and black stockings.

Young girls wore short dresses just below the knee. These were usually frilled and embroidered and generally covered with a white apron, which was sleeveless with a frill at the neck and hem.

BROWN SKIRT

This everyday skirt has a central front panel with a cable trim. The hem is slightly shaped by knitting short rows. Follow the instructions on short row knitting (page 5) and you will be able to avoid the small holes that can occur.

Materials
- A pair of size 19 needles
- 10g ball of DMC cotton perlé 12, in brown, (col 640)

Tension
7sts and 9.5 rows equal 1cm (⅜in), using size 19 needles over st st

Abbreviations
c2f: (cross 2 over the front), slip the next 2 sts onto a spare needle, hold to front of work, k the next 2 sts, then k the 2 sts from spare needle.
c2b: (cross 2 over the back), slip the next 2 sts onto a spare needle, hold to back of work, k the next 2 sts, then k the 2 sts from spare needle.
ssk: [slip 1 st knitwise] twice, then approaching from the left, insert the point of the LH needle into the front of these 2 sts, and knit them tog from this position.
Sl2tog-k1-p2sso: place the point of the RH needle into the next 2 sts as if to k2tog, do not work the sts, but instead, slip them both onto the RH needle, k the next st, then pass the 2 slipped sts, over the knitted st and off the needle.

FRONT
Using size 19 needles cast on 47sts,
1st row: p1, k4, p1, k35, p1, k4, p1,
2nd row: k1, p4, k37, p4, k1,
3rd row: as 1st row,
4th row: k1, p4, k1, p35, k1, p4, k1,
5th row: p1, c2f, p1, k35, p1, c2b, p1,
6th row: as 2nd row,
7th row: as 1st row,
8th row: as 4th row,
9th row: as 1st row,
10th row: as 2nd row,
11th row: as 5th row,
12th row: as 4th row,
13th row: p1, k4, p1, k35, p1, k4, p1,
14th row: k1, p4, k1, p35, k1, p4, k1,

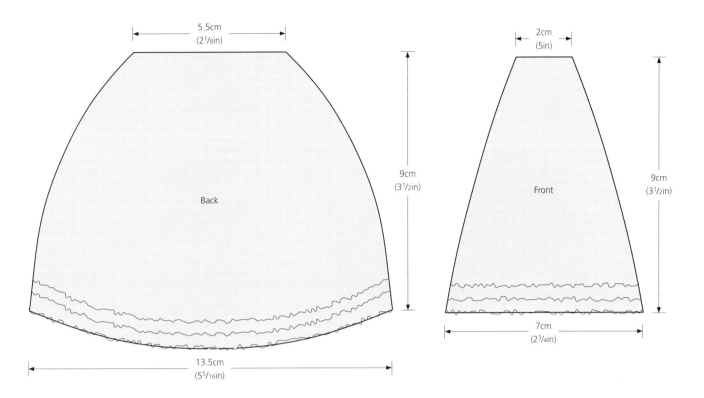

15th row: as 13th row,
16th row: as 14th row,
17th row: p1, c2f, p1, k35, p1, c2b, p1,
18th row: as 14th row,
19th row: p1, k4, p1, k35, p1, k4, p1,
20th row: k1, p4, k1, p35, k1, p4, k1,
21st row: k1, k4, p1, ssk, k31, k2tog, p1, k4, p1,
Cont working in st st with the cable patt as set. At the same time, dec 1 st, as before, at the inside edges of the cable panel on the [foll 8th row], then the [foll 6th row] twice, the [foll 4th row] 8 times, and the [foll 2nd row] 3 times,
Next row: k1, p4, k1, p3, k1, p4, k1,
Next row: p1, k4, p1, sl2tog-k1-p2sso, p1, k4, p1,
patt 1 row, then cast off.

BACK

Using size 19 needles, cast on 95sts,
Next 3 rows: p1, k to last st, p1,
4th row: k1, p to last st, k1
Rep the last 4 rows twice more,
Next row: p1, k89, turn,
Next row: sl1, p84, turn,
Next row: sl1, k74, turn,
Next row: sl1, p64, turn,

Cont in this way working 10 sts less on each row, until you have worked the sl1, p14, row, now turn, sl1, and k to last st, p1,
*Keeping the edge sts in rev. st st as now set, work a further 7 rows st st
Next row: p1, ssk, k to last 3 sts, k2tog, p1,
Rep from * once more,
Working the shaping 1 st in as set, dec 1 st, at each end of the [foll 6th row] twice, the [foll 4th row] 8 times, and the [foll 2nd row] 4 times,
Next row: p1, [p2tog] to end,
Cast off.

TO MAKE UP

Bag out, block and steam the pieces following the instructions in the section on finishing (page 6).

Join the seams, but leave about 2cm (¾in) open at the waist edge of one. Fit to the doll and finish stitching the seam.

Run a gathering thread round the waistline and draw up to fit, making sure that the front is smooth and all the fullness is at the centre back.

CREAM BLOUSE

Materials
- A pair each of size 20, and size 22 needles,
- 50m reel of Gütermann pure silk S303, in cream (col 659)
- Tiny beads for buttons
- Silk bow or rose for decoration

Tension
9sts and 11 rows equal 1cm (⅜in), using size 20 needles over st st

Abbreviations
sl1-k1-psso: slip1, k1, pass the slipped st over and off the needle

FRONT
Using size 20 needles, cast on 58sts and k 3 rows,
Next row: p
Shape centre front
Next row: k26, yfwd, sl1-k1-psso, k2, k2tog, yfwd, k23, turn,
Next row: sl1, p24, k2, p25, turn,
Next row: sl1, k22, yfwd, sl1-k1-psso, k2, k22, turn,
Next row: sl1, p21, k2, p22, turn,
Keeping the 6 centre sts in patt as now set, cont shaping the front hem by working 3sts less on each row, until you have completed the short row of 16sts, now turn, sl1, and k to end,
Beg with a p row work 5 rows straight.
Shape sides
Keeping patt straight, dec 1 st at each end of the

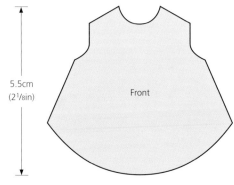

5.5cm
(2⅛in)

Front

next row, then each end of the [foll 6th row] 3 times,
Work 5 rows straight to finish with a WS row, (50sts)

Shape armholes
Cast off 3sts at the beg of the next 2 rows, and 2sts at the beg of the foll 4 rows, then dec 1 st at each end of the next RS row.
Patt 7 rows straight,

Shape shoulders
Next row: cast off 3sts, k10, cast off 6sts, k to end,
Next row: cast off 3 sts, p10, turn,
Cont on these sts only to complete the R shoulder,
Next row: cast off 3sts, k to end,
Next row: cast off 3sts, p to last 2sts, p2tog,
Next row: k2tog, k to end,
p 1 row, then cast off,
Return to the rem sts, with WS facing rejoin yarn and p to end,
Cast off 3sts at the beg of the next 2 rows,
Next row: cast off 3sts, k to last 2sts, k2tog,
Next row: p2tog, p to end,
Cast off rem 3sts.

BACK

Using size 20 needles, cast on 42sts, and k 2 rows,
Beg with a k row, work in st st and inc 1 st. at each end of the 7th row, then each end of the [foll 6th row] 3 times, (50sts),
Work 5 rows without shaping,

Shape armholes
Cast off 3sts at beg of next 2 rows, then 2sts at beg of foll 4 rows, dec 1 st at each end of the foll row,

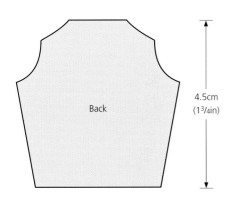

Back

4.5cm
(1³/₄in)

Work back opening and left shoulder
Next row: (WS) p15, k1, turn, cast on 2sts,
Cont on these 18sts only,
Next row, k,
Next row: p, to last 2 sts, k2,
In patt as now set, work 5 rows without shaping,
**Cast off 3sts at the beg of the next row, and
foll 2 alt rows, patt 1 row to finish at armhole edge,
Cast off rem 9sts**.
Work right shoulder
With WS facing rejoin yarn to rem 18sts, k2, p to
end,

Next row: k,
Next row: k2, p to end,
In patt as now set, work 4 rows without shaping,
Work from ** to ** to match left shoulder.

SLEEVES
Using size 22 needles, ***cast on 3sts, k the last
cast-on st. in the normal way, then transfer this
st. back onto the LH needle, knit the same st.
once more, and again return it to the LH
needle*** rep from *** to *** 5 times more,
then cast on 3sts and p1 row, (21sts),
Next row: k,
Next row: p,
Change to size 20 needles,
Cont in st st and inc 1 st at each end of the next
row, and then each end of the foll 4th row] 6
times,
p 1 row, (35sts),
Shape sleeve head
Next row: cast on 3sts, k8, [yfwd, k2tog, k4] 5
times, k1,
Next row: cast on 3sts, p to end,
Next row: cast on 3sts, k to end,
Next row: cast on 3sts, p to end,
Next row: cast on 4sts, k6, [yfwd, k2tog, k4] 7
times, yfwd, k2tog,
Next row: cast on 4sts, p to end,
Work 2 rows st st
Next row: k2tog, k1, [yfwd, k2tog, k4] 8 times,
k2, k2tog,
Work 3 rows st st
Keeping the 8 row eyelet-hole patt correct, dec
1 st. at each end of the next row, then, each end
of the [foll 4th row] 3 times, each end of [every
foll RS row] 6 times, p 1 row,
Cast off 3sts at the beg of the next 4 rows, cast
off rem 21sts.
Work second sleeve to match.

NECK BAND
Using size 22 needles, cast on 5sts, and p 1 row,
1st row: k1, yfwd, sl1-k2tog-psso, yfwd, k1,
2nd row: sl1, p3, k1,
3rd row: k1, yfwd, sl1- k2tog-psso, yfwd, k into
the front, back, then front again of the next st,
4th row: Cast off 2sts, p3, k1,
rep these 4 rows, 9 times more, k 1 row, then
cast off.

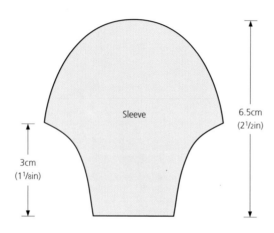

Sleeve

6.5cm
(2½in)

3cm
(1⅛in)

TO MAKE UP

Bag out, block and steam the pieces following the instructions in the
section on finishing (page 6).

Join shoulder and side seams.

Starting about 2cm (¾in) up from the wrist edge (to allow dressing), join
the underarm seam of each sleeve

Gather each sleeve head to fit armhole and stitch into place.

Starting and finishing at the centre back, stitch the straight edge of the
neck-band to the neckline, so that it stands up round the neck.

Put the blouse on the doll and stitch up the back opening. Finish
stitching up the sleeve underarm seams. Run a gathering thread round
the waistline and draw up to fit, making sure that all the gathers are at
the centre front.

Stitch tiny beads down the centre front and the outer edge of the lower
sleeves to resemble button fastenings, and add a bow or small rose to
the neckline.

Pink Skirt

Edwardian skirts should just touch the ground at the front, but be a little bit longer at the back. Check the measurement of your doll with the diagram. If necessary add or subtract a few rows right at the beginning of the knitting.

Materials
- A pair of needles size 19
- 10g ball of DMC cotton perlé 12, in rose pink (col 223)

Tension
7 sts and 10 rows equal 1cm (⅜in), using size 19 needles over st st

Picot Edging
Using size 19 needles, cast on 3sts and p 1 row
1st row: sl1, k2.
2nd row: sl1, k2.
3rd row: sl1, k1, k into f,b,f, of next st.
4th row: Cast off 2sts, k2.
These 4 rows form the patt and are repeated.

Back
Using size 19 needles, cast on 79sts and k 2 rows,
Beg with a k row, work 4 rows in st st
Shape train point.
5th row: k38, sl2tog-k1-p2sso, k38, work 5 rows st st
11th row: k37, sl2tog-k1-p2sso, k37, work 5 rows in st st
17th row: k36, sl2tog-k1-p2sso, k36
18th row: p
Work marker row for picot trim
Next 2 rows: k,
21st row: k35, sl2tog-k1-p2sso, k35,
22nd row: p
Shape train
23rd row: k63, turn,
24th row: p55, turn,
25th row: k47, turn,
Cont in this way working 8sts less on each row until you have worked,
p7, turn.
Next row: k to end,

Next row: p
Shape sides
Cont in st st and work 6 rows straight,
dec 1 st. at each end of the next row,
and the [foll 8th row] twice, the [foll 6th row] twice, [foll 4th row] 5 times, then the foll 4 alt rows. Finish with a wrong side row. (43sts)
Next row: k1, [k2tog] 10 times, k1, [k2tog] to last st. k1,
Cast off rem 23sts.

FRONT

Using size 19 needles, cast on 71sts and k 2 rows,
Beg with a k row, work 18 rows in st st
Place marker row
Next 2 rows: k
Shape hem
21st row: k61, turn,
22nd row: p51, turn,
23rd row: k to end.
24th row: p,
Shape sides
Cont in st st and work 6 rows straight,
now dec 1 st. at each end of the next row, then the [foll 8th row] twice, [each foll 6th row] twice, [each foll 4th row] 5 times, then each end of the

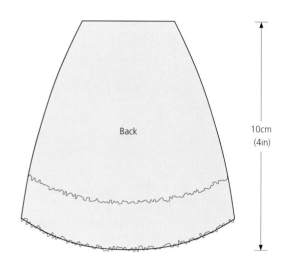

Back
10cm (4in)

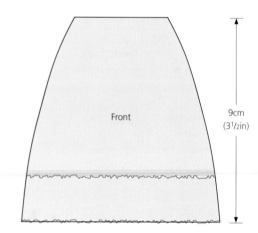

Front
9cm (3½in)

next 2 alt rows. Finish with a p row.
Shape darts
Next row: k2tog, k7, sl1-k2tog-psso, k23, sl1-k2tog-psso, k7, k2tog,
Next row: p to end,
Next row: k2tog, k5, sl1-k2tog-psso, k21, sl1-k2tog-psso, k5, k2tog,
Next row: p,
Next row: k2tog, k3, sl1-k2tog-psso, k19, sl1-k2tog-psso, k3, k2tog,
Next row: p,
Next row: k2tog, k1, sl1-k2tog-psso, k17, sl1-k2tog-psso, k1, k2tog,
Cast off rem 23sts.
Picot edge trim
You will need 2 lengths. For each one work 65 reps of the Picot Edging, but before casting off, check that the length fits round the hem.

TO MAKE UP

Bag out, block and steam the pieces following the instructions in the section on finishing (page 6).

Join the side seams, leaving about 1.5cm (⅝in) open at the waist end of one seam. Stitch each length of trim onto the purl marker rows, by placing RS together and over-sewing the straight edge of the trim to the purl loops. Arrange trim so that picots are towards the hem, and apply steam.

Fit the skirt to your doll and stitch up the remaining 1.5cm (⅝in) of the side seam. Run a gathering thread round the waist-line and draw up to fit, making sure that all the gathers are at the back and that the front is as flat as possible.

Pink Blouse

Materials
- A pair each of size 20, and size 22 needles
- 50m reel of Gütermann pure silk S303, in pink (col 659)

Tension
9sts and 11 rows equal 1cm (⅜in), using size 20 needles over st st

Lace Edging
Using size 22 needles cast on 5sts, and p 1 row,
1st row: sl1, k1, yfwd, k2tog, k1,
2nd row: sl1, k1, yfwd, k2tog, k1,
3rd row: sl1, k1, yfwd, k2tog, k into front, back, front of next st, (7sts),
4th row: Cast off 2sts, k1, yfwd, k2tog, k1,
These 4 rows form the patt and are repeated

Front
Using size 20 needles cast on 58sts and k 3 rows,
Next row: p
Shape centre front
Next row: k55, turn,
Next row: p52, turn,
Next row: k49, turn,
Next row: p46, turn,
Working in st st cont shaping the front by working 3 sts less on each row, as now set, until you have completed the short row of 16sts, now turn and k to end,
Beg with a p row work 5 rows in st st
Shape sides
Keeping patt straight, dec 1 st at each end of the next row, then [each end of foll 6th row] 3 times, (50sts)

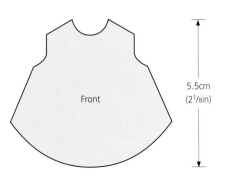

Front

5.5cm
(2⅛in)

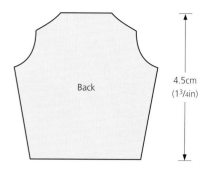

4.5cm
(1³⁄₄in)

Back

Next row: cast off 3 sts, k to end,
Next row: cast off 3 sts, p to last 2sts, p2tog,
Next row: k2tog, k to end,
p 1 row, then cast off,
Return to the rem sts with WS facing rejoin yarn
and p to end,
Cast off 3 sts at the beg of the next 2 rows,
Next row: cast off 3 sts, k to last 2sts, k2tog,
Next row: p2tog, p to end,
Cast off rem 3sts.

BACK

Using size 20 needles, cast on 42sts, and k 2
rows,
Beg with a k row, work in st st, inc 1 st. at each
end of the 7th row, then [each end of the foll
6th row] 3 times, (50sts),
Work 5 rows without shaping.
Shape armholes
Cast off 3sts at beg of next 2 rows, then 2sts at
beg of foll 4 rows, dec 1 st at each end of the foll
row.
Work back opening
Next row: (WS) p15, k1, turn, cast on 2sts,
Cont on these 18sts only and work left shoulder,
Next row: k,
Next row: p, to last 2 sts, k2,
In patt as now set, work 5 rows without shaping,
**Cast off 3sts at the beg of the next row, and
foll 2 alt rows, patt 1 row to finish at armhole
edge,
Cast off rem 9sts**
With WS facing rejoin yarn to rem 18sts, k2, p to
end,
Next row: k,
Next row: k2, p to end,
Keeping patt as now set, work 4 rows without
shaping,
Work from ** to ** to match left shoulder.

Work 5 rows st st to finish with a WS row,
Shape armholes
Cast off 3sts at the beg of the next 2 rows, then
2sts at the beg of the foll 4 rows, then dec 1 st
at each end of the next RS row.
Work 7 rows straight.
Shape shoulders
Next row: cast off 3sts, k10, cast off 6sts, k to end,
Next row: cast off 3 sts, p10, turn,
Cont on these sts only to complete the R
shoulder,

SLEEVES

Using size 22 needles, cast on 20 sts, p1 row,
1st row: k2, *yfwd, sl1-k2tog-psso, yfwd, k1,
rep from * to last 2sts, k2,
2nd and all alt rows: p
3rd row: k2, *k1, yfwd, sl1-k2tog-psso, yfwd,
rep from * to last 2sts,
5th row: k1, k2tog, *yfwd, k1, yfwd, sl1-k2tog-
psso, rep from * to last 5sts, yfwd, k1, yfwd, sl1-
k1-psso, k2,
7th row: k2, k2tog, *yfwd, k1, yfwd, sl1-k2tog-
psso, rep from * to last 4sts, yfwd, k1, yfwd, sl1-
k1-psso, k1,
8th row: p
These 8 rows form the patt; rep them twice more,
25th and 26th rows: p
Shape sleeve head
Change to size 20 needles and work in st st
Next row: k2, [inc into the next st] to last 2sts,
k2, (36sts)
Next row: p
Cast on 3sts at the beg of the next 4 rows, then
4sts at the beg of the foll 2 rows, (56sts),
Work 4 rows without shaping,
Dec 1 st at each end of the next row, then [every
foll 4th row] 4 times, then dec 1st at each end of
every RS row until there are 34sts, finish with a
WS row,
Cast off 3sts at beg of the next 4 rows,
Cast off rem 22 sts,
Work a second sleeve to match.
Lace trim,
For wrist edge work 12 reps of the lace edging,
For elbow trims work 14 reps of the lace edging.

COLLAR

Using size 22 needles, cast on 10sts, and k 2
rows,
1st row: k2, p4, yfwd, k2tog, yfwd, k2,
2nd row: k,
3rd row: k2, p5, yfwd, k2tog, yfwd, k2,
4th row: k10, turn,
5th row: k6, yfwd, k2tog, yfwd, k2,
6th row: k5, p6, turn,
7th row: k1, [yfwd, k2tog] 4 times, yfwd, k2,
8th row: k6, p6, k2,
9th row: k to end,
10th row: cast off 4sts, k to end,
Rep these 10 rows, 17 more times, then k1 row
and cast off.

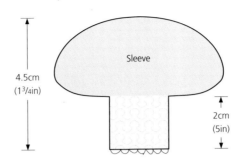

Sleeve

4.5cm (1¾in)

2cm (5in)

NECK BAND

Using size 22 needles, cast on 5sts, and p 1 row,
1st row: sl1, yfwd, sl1-k2tog-psso, yfwd, k1,
2nd row: sl1, p3, k1,
3rd row: sl1, yfwd, sl1- k2tog-psso, yfwd, k into
the front, back, then front again of the next st,
4th row: cast off 2sts, but slip the 1st st rather
than k it, p3, k1,
Rep these 4 rows,11 times more, k 1 row, then
cast off.

TO MAKE UP

Bag out, block and steam the pieces following the instructions in the
section on finishing (page 6).

Join the shoulder and side seams.

Starting about 1cm (⅜in) from the wrist edge, join the underarm seam
of each sleeve. Gather each sleeve-head to fit the armhole and stitch
into place.

Starting and ending at the centre back, stitch the collar to the neckline
gathering it to fit. Then stitch the straight edge of the neck-band to the
neckline, so that it stands up round the neck. Fit the blouse on the doll
and stitch up the back opening, the collar back seam and the neck-band
seam.

Finish closing the sleeve seam.

Run a gathering thread round the waistline and draw up to fit, making
sure that all the fullness is in the centre front.

Add a decorative silk bow or rose to the centre front neck.

Draw-string Purse

Materials

- A pair of size 21 needles
- 50m reel of Gütermann pure silk S303, in brown (col 669)
- Small beads or tassel for decoration

Tension

10sts and 13 rows equal 1cm (⅜in), using size 21 needles over st st

Using size 21 needles cast on 30sts, k 2 rows, then p 1 row,
Inc row: [k1, p1] into each st, (60sts)
Next row: p to end,
Shape bag
1st row: [k2tog, k8] to end,
2nd and all alt rows: p
3rd row: [k2tog, k7] to end
5th row: [k2tog, k6] to end,
Cont to dec in this way until the row, k2tog, k1, has been worked,
Next row: p,
Next row: [k2tog], to end
Next row: p,
Next row: [k2tog] to end,
Break off yarn leaving a long end, thread yarn through rem sts, pull up tightly and fasten off.

Lace Trim

Using size 21 needles, cast on 3sts, and k 1 row,
1st row: k1, yfwd, yrn, k2tog,
2nd row: yfwd, k2, p1, k1,
3rd and 4th rows: k5,
5th row: k1, [yfwd, yrn, k2tog] twice,
6th row: [k2, p1] twice, k1,
7th row: k7,
8th row: cast off 4sts, k to end.
These 8 rows form the patt, work 10 repeats.

Handle

Using size 21 needles, cast on 30sts, then cast them off again.

TO MAKE UP

Join the seam from gathered point to cast-on edge.

Gather the lace trim to fit round the cast-on edge and stitch into place.

Run a gathering thread round the cast-on edge, between the lace and the bag. Pull up tightly and secure ends.

Fold the handle in half lengthways, and stitch into the top of the purse, to form a loop.

Decorate the bag with a tassel or some beads or with some tiny embroidery.

Man's Two-Piece Lounge Suit

This suit is knitted in moss stitch. The fabric is reversible: both right and left jacket fronts can therefore (with some very minor alterations) be knitted from the same instructions. Note that only the left front has a breast pocket. Please read the instructions carefully.

Materials
- A pair each of size 19 and size 20 needles
- Four skeins of DMC Brode Medicis Laine Tapisserie, 100% wool, in rich brown (col 8306)
- Three small buttons or beads

Tension
6sts and 12 rows equal 1cm (⅜in), using size 19 needles over moss st.

Abbreviations
m1: (make 1 stitch), pick up the yarn from previous row which is stretched between the needles, and knit into the back loop of it.
ssk: [slip 1st knitwise] twice, then approaching from the left, insert the point of the LH needle into the front of these 2sts, and then knit them tog from this position.
inc into next st: knit first into the front then the back of the next st.

Jacket

Breast Pocket Lining
Using size 21 needles cast on 7 sts, work 5 rows in st st then dec 1 st at each end of the next row, break off yarn, and leave these sts on the needle.

Pocket Flaps
On the same needle, cast on 5sts, work 4 rows in moss st. break off yarn. Work a second flap on the same needle. (All three pocket bits can be left on the one needle.)

Right and Left Fronts
Using size 19 needles cast on 11sts and k 2 rows,
1st row: k2, m1, p1, [k1, p1] to end,

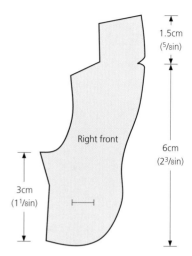

2nd row: [p1, k1] to last 2 sts, k2,
3rd row: k2, m1, [k1, p1] to end,
4th row: p1, [k1, p1] to last 2 sts, k2,
5th row: k2, p1, [k1,p1] to end,
6th row: p1, [k1, p1] to last 2 sts, k2,
7th row: k2, m1,p1, [k1, p1] to end,
8th row: [p1, k1] to last 2 sts k2,
9th row: k2, [k1, p1] to end,
10th row: [p1, k1] to last 2sts, k2,
11th row: k2, m1, [k1, p1] to end,
12th row: [k1, p1] to last 2sts, k2,
Keeping moss st. patt and edge sts as now set, patt 2 rows without shaping. Dec 1 st. at the end of the next row and patt 1 row.

RIGHT FRONT ONLY

Add pocket flap,
17th row: k2, m1, p1, k1, p1, k1, place pocket flap on the front of work, with spare needle parallel to LH needle and points matching, [ktog 1 st. from each needle], 5 times, then k1, p2tog, to finish row.

LEFT FRONT ONLY

Add pocket flap
17th row: k2, m1, [p1, k1] twice, place pocket flap to the back of the work, with the spare needle behind and parallel to the LH needle, [ptog, 1 st. from each needle] 5 times, k1, p2tog.

BOTH FRONTS

Next 5 rows: cont in patt without shaping,
23rd row: k2, m1, patt to last st, inc into next st. Keeping patt correct, inc 1 st. at the end of the

[foll 4th row.} twice, then
patt 4 rows without shaping.

Shape armhole
Cast off 2sts at beg of next row, and foll 2 alt
rows, to finish at centre front edge, (12sts)
Next row: k2, m1, patt to end,
Next 5 rows: cont in patt without shaping,
6th row: k2, m1, patt to end,

RIGHT FRONT ONLY

Rep the last 6 rows, 3 more times, (17sts)

LEFT FRONT ONLY

Next row: patt 3sts, p5, patt to end,
Next row: patt 6, cast off 5, patt to end,
Next row: patt 3, replace the cast off sts, by patt
across the pocket lining sts from spare needle (RS
facing), then patt to end to finish the row.
Next 2 rows: patt with out shaping,
Next row: k2, m1, patt to end,
Next 5 rows: patt without shaping,
Next row: k2, m1, patt to end,
Rep the last 6 rows once more. (17sts)

BOTH FRONTS

Shape shoulder and lapel
Cast off 2sts at the beg of next row, and patt to
end,
Next row: cast off 3sts, return the st now on the
RH needle back to the LH needle, cast on 4sts, k2,
p1, k2tog, patt to end,
Keeping patt correct, cast off 2sts at the beg of
the next row, and 3sts at the beg of foll alt row,
(10sts)

Shape collar
Still keeping the centre front edge sts in garter st.
patt for 4 rows
Next row: patt to last 3sts, turn, sl1, patt to end,
Patt 10 rows straight then cast off.

BACK

Using size 19 needles cast on 31sts, and k 2 rows,
1st row: k1, [p1, k1] to end,
Rep this row 12 more times,
Keeping patt as set dec 1 st. at each end of the
next row, and then the foll alt row,
Work straight for 5 more rows,
inc 1 st at each end of the next row, and the [foll
4th row] twice, then patt 1 row,

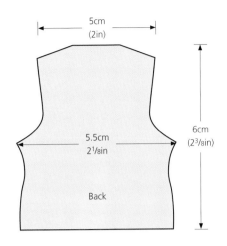

5cm
(2in)

6cm
(2³⁄₈in)

5.5cm
2¹⁄₈in

Back

Next row: k1, patt 15, m1, patt 1, m1, patt to end,
Patt 1 more row.

Shape armholes
Cast off 2sts at the beg of the next 2 rows, then
dec 1 st. at each end of the next 4 rows,
Next row: patt 11, m1, patt 1, m1, patt to end,
Keeping patt as set, patt 5 rows without shaping,
Next row: patt 12, m1, patt 1, m1, patt to end,
Keeping patt as set, patt for 5 more rows,
Next row: patt 13, m1, patt 1, m1, patt to end,
Patt 13 rows without shaping,

Shape shoulders,
Next row: patt to last 3sts, turn,
Next row: sl1, patt to last 3sts, turn,
Next row: sl1, patt 5, cast off 10, patt 2, turn,
Next row: sl1, patt 2, turn, cast off 9sts,
At neck edge, rejoin yarn to rem sts, patt 3, turn,
sl1, patt 2, turn, cast off.

SLEEVES

Using size 19 needles, cast on 26sts, and k 2 rows,
Work in moss st for 10 rows

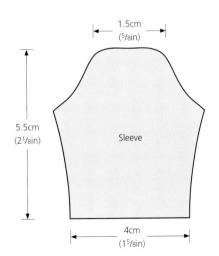

1.5cm
(⁵⁄₈in)

5.5cm
(2¹⁄₈in)

Sleeve

4cm
(1⁵⁄₈in)

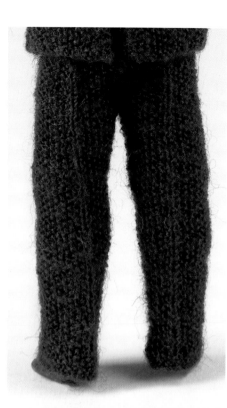

Shape sides

Inc 1 st. at each end of the next row, then [each end of the foll 12th row] twice,
Work a further 5 rows without shaping,

Shape sleeve head

Cast off 2sts at beg of next 4 rows, then dec 1 st at each end of the foll 3rd row, each end of the [foll 4th row] twice, and each end of the [foll alt row] 3 times, patt 1 row.
Cast off rem 12sts.

TROUSERS

LEFT LEG

Using size 19 needles cast on 33sts and knit 4 rows

1st row: p1, [k1, p1] to end,

2nd row: p1,[k1, p1] 3 times, p1, [p1, k1] 8 times, p2, [p1, k1] 3 times, p1,
These 2 rows form the patt
Cont in patt for a further 48 rows,
Keeping patt correct, inc 1 st at each end of the next row, then each end of the [foll 8th row] 3 times, then patt 3 rows without shaping.

Shape crotch

Cast off 3sts at the beg of the next 2 rows, and 2sts at the beg of foll 2 rows,   (31sts)
Cont in patt without shaping for 26 rows.
Cast off.
Work a second leg to match.

TO MAKE UP

Bag out, block and steam the pieces following the instructions in the section on finishing (page 6).

Jacket. At the back vent fold the right edge over the left, and secure the cast off sts to the underside.

Join the shoulder seams.

Join the collar centre-back seam, and stitch the collar to the neckline, secure a very short length of the side edge of the collar to the lapel cast-off sts to form a 'V' shape

Slip-stitch the pocket lining into place.

Join side seams.

Join the underarm seam of each sleeve and stitch the sleeves into place.

Trousers. Join the inside leg seam of each leg. Join the centre back and centre front seams. Run a gathering thread round the waistline and draw up to fit..

Add three small beads or buttons to the right front of the jacket.

Knit a tiny square handkerchief in white silk or cotton and pop it into the breast pocket..

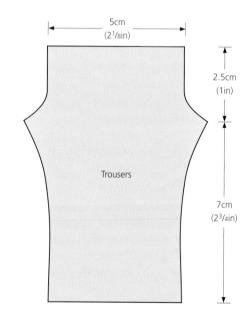

5cm
(2¹⁄₈in)

2.5cm
(1in)

Trousers

7cm
(2³⁄₄in)

FAIR ISLE WAISTCOAT

This neat little waistcoat matches the lounge suit, but it can of course be knitted in any colour you choose.

Materials

- A pair each of size 19 and size 20 needles
- Skein of DMC Broder Medicis, tapestry wool in dark brown, (col 8306)
- Skein of DMC Broder Medicis, tapestry wool in ginger brown, (col 8300)
- Small amount of Gütermann pure silk, S303, in a matching shade for the back
- Four tiny beads for buttons

Tension:

9.5sts and 8 rows equal 1cm (⅜in) using size 19 needles and wool over Fair Isle pattern,
9sts and 11 rows equal 1cm (⅜in) using size 20 needles and silk over st st

Abbreviations:

M = main yarn, dark brown
C = contrast col ginger brown

RIGHT FRONT

Using size 19 needles and M yarn cast on16sts and k 1 row
1st row: M:k2, [C:k1, M:k1] to end,
2nd row: [C:p1, M:p1] to last 2sts, M:k2,
These 2 rows set the tweed patt
3rd row: M:k2, inc into next st, patt to end,
4th row: patt to last 3sts, inc into the next st. M:k2,
Rep the last 2 rows once more, (20sts)
Work pocket bag
Next row: M:k2, patt 5, M:p4, turn,
Next row: M:p4, turn,
Cont on these 4sts and using M, beg with a k row work 8 rows in st st turn, now using both yarns complete the row in patt.
Cont in tweed patt and inc 1 st. at the armhole edge of the next row, and then [the foll 4th row] twice, (23sts)
Patt 1 row without shaping, to finish at armhole edge,
Shape armhole
Cast off 3sts at beg of the next row and foll alt row, then dec 1 st at the same edge of foll alt

row,
Next 2 rows: M:k2, patt to last 2sts, M:k2, to finish at neck edge,
Shape neck
Next row: M:k2, M:ssk, patt to last 2sts, M:k2
Next row: M:k2, patt to last 4sts, M:p2tog, M:k2
Rep the last 2 rows, 3 times more,
Keeping armhole and front edge band as set, patt 2 rows without shaping, to finish at neck edge,
Shape shoulder

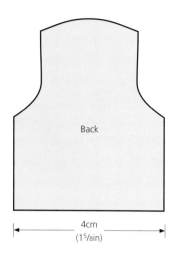

Back

4cm
(1⁵/₈in)

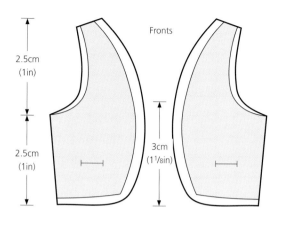

Fronts

2.5cm
(1in)

2.5cm
(1in)

3cm
(1¹/₈in)

Next row: patt to last 3sts, turn, sl1, patt to end,
Next row: M:k2, turn, sl1, k1,
Cast off.

LEFT FRONT

Using size 19 needles and M yarn, cast on 16sts
and k 1 row,
1st row: [M:k1, C:k1] to last 2sts, M:k2
2nd row: M:k2, [M:p1, C:p1] to end,
These 2 rows set the tweed patt
3rd row: patt to last 3sts, inc into next st, M:k2,
4th row: M:k2, inc into next st, patt to end,
Rep the last 2 rows once more, (20sts)
then patt 1 row to finish at centre front edge,
Work pocket bag,
Next row: M:k2, patt 5sts, M:k4 turn. Cont on
these 4sts only, using M yarn, beg with a k row
and work 9 rows in st st, turn, and using both

yarns, complete the row in patt
Cont in tweed patt and inc 1 st at the armhole
edge of the next row, and [the foll 4th row]
twice, (23sts)
Patt 1 row without shaping, to finish at armhole
edge,
Shape armhole,
Cast off 3sts at the beg of the next row and foll
alt row, then dec 1 st at the same edge of the foll
alt row,
Next row: M:k2, patt to last 2sts, M:k2
Shape neck
Next row: M:k2, patt to last 4sts, k2tog, M:k2
Next row: M:k2, p2tog, patt to last 2sts, M:k2
Rep the last 2 rows, 3 times more, then patt 1
row to finish at the neck edge.
Shape shoulder
Next row: patt to last 3 turn, sl1, patt to end,
Next row: M:k2, turn, sl1, k1,
Cast off.

BACK

Using size 20 needles and silk thread, cast on
36sts and k 2 rows,
Beg with a k row and work 26 rows in st st
Shape armholes
Cast off 2sts at the beg of the next 4 rows, then
work 20 rows without shaping,
Shape shoulders
Next row: k to last 5sts, turn, sl1, p 3, cast off
10, k the next 3sts, turn,
Next row: k4, turn, cast off rem 9sts,
With RS facing rejoin yarn to rem sts, k to end,
Cast off.

TO MAKE UP

Bag out, block and steam the pieces following the instructions in the
section on finishing (page 6).

Complete the pockets by stitching together the sides of each fold to
form a little bag. Steam to make neat and flat.

Join shoulder and side seams. (Stitching with the silk thread will make
a finer seam.) Fit the waistcoat onto the doll, overlap the fronts, left over
right, and stitch on the buttons – stitching through both layers.

MAN'S SHIRT AND TIE

Instructions are given for a normal length shirt and a shorter version.

If the shirt is to be worn under a jacket you can avoid that bulky look by making the short (half shirt) version, omitting the sleeves, and adding the separate cuffs which can be stitched to the inside of the jacket sleeves.

Choose either a normal long tie or a bow tie: they are both very simple and quick to knit.

Materials

❀ A pair each of size 20 and size 21 needles
❀ 50m reel of Gütermann pure silk, S303, in white (col 800)
❀ A small amount of Gütermann pure silk, S303, in mustard (col 448) or other contrast colour for the tie

Tension

9sts and 11 rows equal 1cm (⅜in), using size 20 needles over st st

SHIRT

BACK

Using size 21 needles and white thread, cast on 50sts, and k 1 row,
Change to size 20 needles,
Beg with a k row work 40 rows in st st (or 20 rows for half shirt to go under suit),
Shape armholes

Cast off 3sts at the beg of the next 2 rows, then 2sts at the beg of the foll 4 rows,
Divide to complete right back
Next row: patt 19sts, turn, k2, patt to end,
Keeping the 2sts at centre back in g st work 17 rows straight, to finish at the neck edge,
**Shape shoulder
Next row: patt 16, turn, sl1, patt to end,
Next row: patt 13, turn, sl1, patt to end,
Next row: patt 9, turn, sl1, patt to end**
Patt 1 row, then cast off.

Work L back and shoulder
Return to rem sts, with RS facing rejoin yarn, cast on 2sts, k to end,
Next row: p to last 2sts, k2,
Keeping the 2sts at centre back in g st
Work 18 rows straight, to finish at the neck edge.
Work from ** to** to match R shoulder, then cast off.

FRONT

Using size 20 needles and white, cast on 50sts, and k 1 row,
1st row: k, to end,
2nd row: p24, k2, p24,
These 2 rows form the patt
Cont in patt for a further 38 rows, or 18 rows for the half shirt
Shape armholes
Cast off 3sts at the beg of the next 2 rows, then 2sts at the beg of the foll 4 rows,
Work 16 rows without shaping,

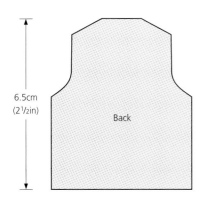

Back

6.5cm
(2½in)

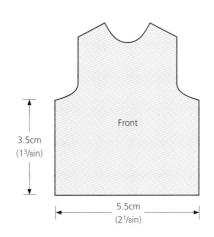

Front

3.5cm
(1⅜in)

5.5cm
(2⅛in)

Shape neck

k14, cast off 8sts, k to end,

Next row: p14, turn,

Cont on these sts only to shape the R neck and shoulder,

Cast off 2sts, at beg of next row, then patt the foll row,

Next row: cast off 2sts, patt 4, turn, sl1, patt to end, then cast off.

With WS facing rejoin yarn to rem sts, Cast off 2sts at beg of next row, and patt the foll row

Next row: cast off 2sts, patt 4, turn, sl1, patt to end, patt 1 row, then cast off.

SLEEVES

Using size 21 needles cast on 28sts, ***work 7 rows in st st then k the next WS row, rep from * once more

Change to size 20 needles,

Next row: k3, [inc into next st.] to last 3 sts, k3, (50sts)**

Beg with a p row, cont in st st for 37 more rows,

Shape sleeve head

Cast off 3sts at the beg of the next 4 rows,

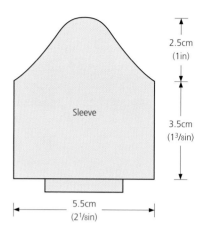

Sleeve

2.5cm (1in)

3.5cm (1³/₈in)

5.5cm (2¹/₈in)

Dec 1 st. at each end of the next row, and [each end of the foll 4th row] 3 times, [the foll alt row] 3 times, [every row] 7 times, then cast off the rem 10sts.

Work a second sleeve to match.

CUFFS ONLY

Follow instructions for the sleeve working from ** to **

Beg with a p row, work 6 rows in st st then cast off knit-wise.

Work second cuff to match.

COLLAR

Using size 21 needles and contrast (tie colour) yarn, cast on 42sts, and work 2 rows in moss st. Change to white (shirt) yarn, beg with a k row, work 4 rows in st st,

Next row: k21 turn, sl1, p to end,

Cont in st st on these 21sts only for 3 more rows

Next row: k, to form fold line,

Beg with a k row, work 5 rows st st cast off,

With RS facing, rejoin yarn to rem sts, beg with a k row, work 5 rows st st, k 1 row to form fold line, then another 5 rows st st. Cast off.

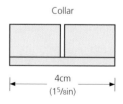

Collar

4cm (1⁵/₈in)

TIE

Using size 21 needles and the contrast yarn, cast on 4sts, work in moss st until knitting measures about 3cms for the long tie, or 1.5cms for a bow tie, then cast off.

TO MAKE UP

Join shoulder seams.

Fold each half of the collar along its fold line and slip-stitch in place. Slip-stitch each double short end from the right side to make tidy. For the winged collar, fold down the centre front corners and secure with a couple of stitches. Stitch the coloured tie edge of the collar to the neckline, so that it stands up round the neck. Join the shirt side seams. Join each sleeve seam. Fold cuff on fold line and stitch. Stitch sleeves in place.

To make the bow tie, fold the length of knitting in half and join the two narrow edges. Fold so that the seam is in the centre, and wrap a double length of silk yarn round the centre until it looks like a knot. Secure the ends and stitch onto the collar.

To make the long tie, twist or tie a knot into one end of the strip of knitting and stitch to the collar.

Short cuffs. From the right side, push the cuffs inside the jacket sleeve. When you are happy with the amount of cuff showing, tack securely in place, remembering to match the seams. Turn the sleeve inside out, and slip-stitch the cast-off edge of the cuff to the inside of the sleeve.

Stitch a small bead cuff-link to each cuff at the little finger position.

Girl's Blue Dress
To fit a 10cm (4 inch) Doll

Materials
- A pair each of size 21 and size 20 needles
- 100m reel of Gütermann pure silk S303, in blue denim (col 322)
- A small amount of Gütermann pure silk S303 in lilac, (col 391)

Tension
9sts and 11 rows equal 1cm (⅜in), using size 20 needles over st st

Abbreviations
Sl2tog-k1-p2sso, place the point of the RH needle into the next 2 sts as if to k2tog, do not work them, but instead, slip them both onto the RH needle, k the next st., then pass the 2 slipped sts over the knitted st and off the needle

FRONT
*Using size 21 needles and contrast yarn, cast on 84sts and p 2 rows,
Change to size 20 needles and Main yarn. Beg with a k row, work 10 rows in st st
Work stripes
Next 2 rows: Contrast yarn k to end,
Next row: Main yarn k to end,
Next row: Main yarn p to end,
Rep the last 4 rows, twice more*
In main yarn only, cont in st st for a further 32 rows,
Next row: [sl2tog-k1-p2sso] to end, (28sts)
Change to size 21 needles and contrast yarn, and p 3 rows,
Work bodice
Change back to size 20 needles and Main yarn and k 1 row,
Next row: k1, [p1, k4] 5 times, p1, k1,
Next row: p1, [k1, p4] 5 times, k1, p1,
Next row: k1, [p1, k4] 5 times, p1, k1,
The last 2 rows form the rib patt, cont in patt and dec 1 st at each end of the next 2 rows, work 8 rows without shaping, then inc 1 st at each end of the next row, work 3 rows straight,
Shape neck and shoulders
Next row: patt 12, cast off 2, patt to end,
Next row: patt 10, k2tog, turn,

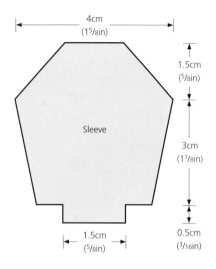

Sleeve

4cm
(1⁵/₈in)

1.5cm
(⁵/₈in)

3cm
(1¹/₈in)

1.5cm
(⁵/₈in)

0.5cm
(³/₁₆in)

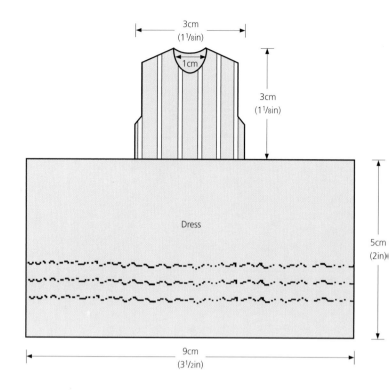

Dress

3cm
(1¹/₈in)

1cm

3cm
(1¹/₈in)

5cm
(2in)

9cm
(3¹/₂in)

Cont on these 11sts only, and dec 1 st. at the neck edge of the next 2 rows,
Next row: patt 5, turn, sl1, patt to end,
Next row: patt to end. Cast off.
Return to rem sts with WS facing rejoin yarn, working in patt dec 1 st at the neck edge of the next 3 rows, then patt 1 row straight,
Next row: patt 5, turn, sl1, patt to end. Cast off.

BACK

Rep from * to * to match the front,
In main yarn only, cont in st st for
22 rows,
Divide to complete R back
Next row: k43, turn, k2, p to end,
Cont on these 43sts only to complete the R back, work in st st but keep the 2 centre back sts in garter st for 8 more rows,
Next row: [sl2tog-k1-p2sso] to last st k1, (15sts)
Change to size 21 needles and contrast yarn
Next row: k2, p to end,
Next row: p to last 2sts, k2,
Next row: k2, p to end,
Change back to size 20 needles and main yarn and k 1 row,

Next row: k3, [p1, k4] twice, p1, k1,
Next row: p1, k1, [p4, k1] twice, p1, k2,
Next row: k3, [p1, k4] twice, p1, k1,
Keeping patt correct, dec 1 st at the armhole edge of the next 2 rows, then work 17 more rows without shaping, to finish at the centre back edge,
Shape neck and shoulders.
Cast off 5sts, patt 5, turn, sl1, patt to end. Cast off.
Complete L back
With RS facing, return to rem sts, rejoin yarn, cast on 2sts and k to end,
Next row: p to last 2sts, k2,
Keeping the 2 centre back sts in garter st work 8 rows in st st,
Next row: K1, [sl2tog-k1-p2sso] to end,
Change to size 21 needles and contrast yarn,
Next row: p to last 2sts, k2,
Next row: k2, p to end,
Next row: p to last 2sts, k2,
Change back to size 20 needles and main yarn and k 1 row,
Next row: k1, [p1, k4] twice, p1, k3,
Next row: k2, p1, [k1, p4] twice, k1, p1,
Next row: k1, [p1, k4] twice, p1, k3,
Keeping patt correct dec 1 st at the armhole edge of the next 2 rows,

patt 16 rows without shaping to finish at the neck edge,
Next row: cast off 5sts, patt 5, turn, sl1 patt to end, patt 1 row. Cast off.

SLEEVES

Using size 21 needles and contrast yarn, cast on 14sts, and k 4 rows,
Change to size 20 needles and main yarn,
Next row: [inc once into next st] to end (28sts),
Beg with a p row, work in st st and increase 1 st at each end of every [foll 6th row] 4 times, work 3 rows without shaping, (36sts)
Shape sleeve head
Dec 1 st at each end of the next 14 rows,
Cast off rem 8sts.
Work a second sleeve to match.

COLLAR

Using size 21 needles, and contrast yarn, cast on 4 sts,
1st row: k1, p3,
2nd row: k1, yfwd, k1 tbl, yfwd, sl1-k1-psso,
3rd row: k1, p2, [k1, p1, k1, p1] into next st, p1,
4th row: cast off 4sts, k1, yfwd, sl1-k1-psso,
Repeat these 4 rows, 3 times more. Cast off,
Work a second piece to match.

TO MAKE UP

Bag out, block and steam the pieces following the instructions in the section on finishing (page 6).

Join shoulder seams.

Beginning and ending at the centre back, stitch the collar to the neckline.

Join the dress side seams.

Join the sleeve seams and stitch the sleeves into place, slightly easing in the sleeve-head as you work.

Girl's White Pinafore

The bottom half of the petticoat is a sideways knitted length of lace edging. This is stitched onto the cast-on edge of the main body of the garment. The pattern for the edging is easier to knit than the long instructions may suggest, but it might be a good idea to organise some quiet uninterrupted time for this task.

Materials

- A pair each of size 20 and size 21 needles
- 100m reel of Gütermann pure silk S303, in white (col 800)

Tension

9sts and 11 rows equal 1cm (⅜in) using size 20 needles over st st

Abbreviations

ssk: [slip 1st knitwise] twice, then approaching from the left, insert the point of the LH needle into the front of these 2sts, and then knit them tog from this position
sl1-k2tog-psso: slip 1st, k2tog, pass the slipped stitch over and off the needle,
2yo: wrap the yarn twice round the needle to make 2 new sts
g st: (garter stitch) knit every row

Pinafore

Bottom Half

The foll 20 rows form the patt and are repeated 9 times, when you have the 9 points, k1 row, then cast off.

Using size 20 needles cast on 18sts, and k 1 row,
1st row: k3, yfwd, k2tog, yfwd, k1, k2tog, 2yfwd, [k2tog] twice, yfwd, k1, k2tog, yfwd, k2tog, k1,
2nd row: k2, yfwd, k1, k2tog, yfwd, k4, p1, k2tog, yfwd, k3, yfwd, k2tog, k1,

3rd row: k3, yfwd, k2tog, k2, yfwd, [k2tog] twice, 2yfwd, k2tog, k1, yfwd, k2tog, k1, yfwd, k2,
4th row: k2, yfwd, k1, k2tog, yfwd, k4, p1, k2tog, yfwd, k1, k2tog, k2, yfwd, k2tog, k1,
5th row: k3, yfwd, k2tog, k3, yfwd, [k2tog] twice, 2yfwd, [k2tog, k1, yfwd] twice, k2,
6th row: k2, yfwd, k1, k2tog, yfwd, k4, p1, k2tog, yfwd, k1, yfwd, k2tog, k3, yfwd, k2tog, k1,
7th row: k3, yfwd, [k2tog] twice, yfwd, k3, yfwd, [k2tog] twice, 2yfwd, [k2tog, k1, yfwd] twice, k2,
8th row: k2, yfwd, k1, k2tog, yfwd, k4, p1, k2tog, yfwd, k5, [yfwd, k2tog, k1] twice,
9th row: k3, yfwd, k2tog, k1, yfwd, k2tog, k1, k2tog, yfwd, k1, yfwd, [k2tog] twice, 2yfwd, [k2tog, k1, yfwd] twice, k2,
10th row: k2, yfwd, k1, k2tog, yfwd, k4, p1, k2tog, yfwd, k3, yfwd, sl1-k2tog-psso, yfwd, k4, yfwd, k2tog, k1,
11th row: k3, yfwd, k2tog, k2, k2tog, yfwd, k5, yfwd, [k2tog] twice, 2yfwd, [k2tog, k1, yfwd] twice, k2,
12th row: k1, k2tog, yfwd, k2tog, k1, yfwd, k2tog, k1, p1, k3, yfwd, k2tog, k1, k2tog, yfwd, k1, yfwd, k2tog, k3, yfwd, k2tog, k1,
13th row: k3, yfwd, [k2tog] twice, yfwd, k3, yfwd, sl1-k2tog-psso, yfwd, k1, k2tog, 2yfwd, [k2tog] twice, yfwd, k1, k2tog, yfwd, k2tog, k1,
14th row: k1, k2tog, yfwd, k2tog, k1, yfwd, k2tog, k1, p1, k3, yfwd, k2tog, k4, [yfwd, k2tog, k1] twice,
15th row: k3, yfwd, k2tog, k1, yfwd, k2tog, k1, k2tog, yfwd, k1, k2tog, 2yfwd, [k2tog] twice, yfwd, k1, k2tog, yfwd, k2tog, k1,
16th row: k1, k2tog, yfwd, k2tog, k1, yfwd, k2tog, k1, p1, k3, yfwd, sl1-k2tog-psso, yfwd, k4, yfwd, k2tog, k1,
17th row: k3, yfwd, k2tog, k2, k2tog, yfwd, k1, k2tog, 2yfwd, [k2tog] twice, yfwd, k1, k2tog, yfwd, k2tog, k1,
18th row: k1, k2tog, yfwd, k2tog, k1, yfwd, k2tog, k1, p1, k3, yfwd, k2tog, k3, yfwd, k2tog, k1,
19th row: k3, yfwd, [k2tog] twice, yfwd, k1, k2tog, 2yfwd, [k2tog] twice, yfwd, k1, k2tog, yfwd, k2tog, k1,
20th row: k1, k2tog, yfwd, k2tog, k1, yfwd, k2tog, k1, p1, k3, [yfwd, k2tog, k1] twice.

Main Body

Using size 20 needles cast on 140sts, p1 row,

1st row: k4, *yfwd, ssk, k8, rep from * to end last rep k4, instead of k8,

2nd row and all alt rows: k2, p to last 2sts, k2

3rd row: k2, *k2tog, yfwd, k1, yfwd, ssk, k5, rep from * to end last rep k3 instead of k5,

5th row: as 1st row,

7th and 9th row: k,

11th row: k9, *yfwd, ssk, k8, rep from * to end last rep k9 instead of k8,

13th row: k7, *k2tog, yfwd, k1, yfwd, ssk, k5, rep from * to end last rep k3 instead of k5,

14th row: k2, p to last 2sts, k2,

Rep rows 1 to 8,

Shape armholes

Next row: k32, cast off 6, k the next 63sts, cast off 6, k to end,

Next row: k32, turn,

Cont on these sts only to complete the L back, work 2 rows st st then patt as folls,

1st row: k6, *yfwd, ssk, k8, rep from * to end last rep k4 instead of k8,

2nd and 4th rows: k2, p to last 2sts k2,

3rd row: k4, *k2tog, yfwd, k1, yfwd, ssk, k5, rep from * to end last rep k3 instead of k5,

5th row: as 1st row,

Work 3 rows st st,

Next row: [sl2tog-k1-p2sso] to last 2sts, k2,

Cast off.

With WS facing return to rem sts and rejoin yarn,

Next row: k2, p60, k2, turn, cont on these 64sts only to complete the front,

Work 2 rows st st then patt as folls.

1st row: k6, *yfwd, ssk, k8, rep from * to end last rep k6 instead of k8

2nd and 4th rows: k2, p to last 2sts, k2

3rd row: k4, *k2tog, yfwd, k1, yfwd, ssk, k5, rep from * to end

5th row: as 1st row,

Work 3 rows st st

Next row: k2tog, [sl2tog-k1-p2sso] to last 2sts, k2tog,

Next row: k4, cast off 14, k4,

Next row: k4, turn, on these last 4sts only work 6 rows in g st then cast off.

With WS facing return to the rem 4sts, rejoin yarn and work 7 rows g st and cast off.

With WS facing rejoin yarn to the rem 32sts, beg with a p row work 3 rows in st st then patt as folls.

1st row: k4, *yfwd, ssk, k8, rep from * to end last rep k6 instead of k8

2nd and 4th rows: k2, p to last 2sts, k2

3rd row: k2, *k2tog, yfwd, k1, yfwd, ssk, k5, rep from * to end

5th row: as 1st row,

Work 3 rows st st

Next row: k2, [sl2tog-k1-p2sso] to end,

Cast off.

Collar

Using size 21 needles cast on 7sts and p 1 row,

Preparation row: k3, yfwd, k2tog, 2yfwd, k2

1st row: k3, p1, k2, yfwd, k2tog, k1,

2nd row: k3, yfwd, k2tog, k4,

3rd row: cast off 2sts, k the next 3, turn,

4th row: yfwd, k2tog, 2yfwd, k2

These 4 rows form the patt; rep them until you have 26 points, then k 1 row and cast off.

TO MAKE UP

Bag out, block and steam the pieces following the instructions in the section on finishing (page 6).

Place the RS together and carefully over-sew the long straight edge of the border to the cast-on edge of the pinafore main body. Be particularly careful to ease-in the border to fit the cast-on edge, rather than stretching the cast-on edge to fit the border.

Stitch each shoulder strap to the back cast-off edge. Beginning at the centre back, place the WS of the collar on the RS of the pinafore and invisibly stitch on the collar. Work along the back cast-off edge, over the shoulder strap then along the front cast-off sts, to finish at the centre back. Make sure that you ease-on the collar to fit the neck, and do not stretch the neck edge of the pinafore to fit the collar.

BOY'S NORFOLK JACKET AND KNICKERBOCKERS

Materials
- A pair each of size 19 and size 20 needles
- Three skeins of DMC Broderi Medicis Laine Tapesserie in sage green (col 8309)
- 50m reel of Gütermann pure silk S303, in cream (col 802)

Tension
7sts and 11 rows equal 1cm (⅜in) using size 19 needles over st st

JACKET

BACK
Using size 20 needles and green wool, cast on 25sts, and k 3 rows,
Change to size 19 needles, beg with a k row and work 2 rows in st st. Cont in st st as set, and dec 1 st at each end of the next row and the foll 4th row, work 3 rows straight, now inc 1 st at each end of the next row and the foll 4th row, (25sts).
Cont without shaping for 5 more rows,

Shape armholes
Dec 1 st at each end of the next 3 rows, then work straight for 15 rows,

Shape shoulders
Next row: k16sts, turn,
Next row: p4, cast off 5, p the next 3sts, turn,
Next row: k2, k2tog, turn,
Next row: cast off 6sts.
Return to rem sts with WS facing rejoin yarn, k 2tog, k2, then cast off.

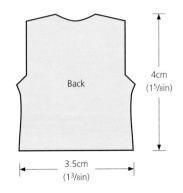

Back

4cm
(1⁵/₈in)

3.5cm
(1³/₈in)

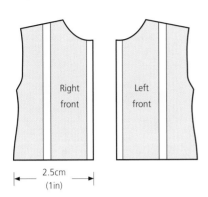

2.5cm
(1in)

RIGHT FRONT

Using size 20 needles and green wool, cast on18sts and k 3 rows,
Change to size 19 needles,
1st row: k8, p2, k to end,
2nd row: p8, k2, p to last 3sts, k3,
These 2 rows form the patt and are used throughout. Keeping patt as set dec 1 st at the end of the next row and the foll 4th row.
Work 3 rows straight, then inc 1 st at the end of the next row and the foll 4th row.
Work 5 rows straight,
Shape armholes
Dec 1 st at the end of the next row and the same edge of the foll 2 rows.
Work straight for 13 more rows to finish at neck edge,
Shape neck
Cast off 4sts at the beg of next row, and dec 1 st at the end of the foll row,
Next row: k2tog, k4, turn,
Next row: p3, p2tog, turn,
Cast off 8sts.

LEFT FRONT

Using size 20 needles and green wool, cast on 18sts and k 3 rows,
Change to size 19 needles,
1st row: k8, p2, k to end,
2nd row: k3, p5, k2, p to end,
These 2 rows form the patt and are used throughout, keeping patt as set dec 1 st at the beg of the next row and the foll 4th row,
Work 3 rows straight, then inc 1 st at the beg of the next row and the foll 4th row,
Work 5 rows straight,
Shape armholes
Dec 1 st at the beg of the next row and the same edge of the foll 2 rows,

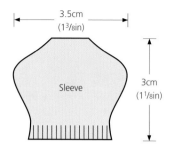

3.5cm
(1³/₈in)

Sleeve

3cm
(1¹/₈in)

Work straight for 12 more rows to finish at neck edge.

Shape neck
Cast off 4sts, at the beg of next row, and dec 1 st at the end of the foll row,
Next row: p2tog, p4, turn,
Next row: k3, k2tog, turn,
Cast off 8sts.

SLEEVES

Using size 20 needles and green wool, cast on 18sts, and k 3 rows,
Change to size 19 needles, beg with a k row and work in st st as folls, inc 1 st at each end of the next row, then each end of [the foll 6th row] 3 times, finish with a WS row, (26sts)
Shape top
Dec 1 st at each end of every row until 6 sts rem, cast off.
Work a second sleeve to match.

BELT

Using size 20 needles and green wool cast on 3 sts,

Next row: k1, p1, k1,
Rep this row until belt measures 6cms (2⅜in),
Next row: sl1-k2tog-psso, fasten off.

COLLAR

Note that p side is the RS,
Using size 20 needles and silk, cast on 12sts and k 1 row,
1st row: k,
2nd row: k2, p to end,
3rd row: k10, turn,
4th row: sl1, p to end,
Rep these 4 rows, 18 times more, k 2 rows and cast off.

Collar

1cm
(³/₈in)

KNICKERBOCKERS

LEG

Using size 20 needles and green wool cast on 15sts, work in k1, p1, rib for 4 rows,
Change to size 19 needles,
Inc row: k twice into each st (30sts)
Next row: p,
Cont in st st for 20 more rows,
Cast off 2 sts at the beg of the next 4 rows, then cont straight for 12 more rows,
Cast off.
Work a second leg to match.

TO MAKE UP

Bag out, block and steam the pieces following the instructions in the section on finishing (page 6).

Stitch jacket shoulder and side seams.

Join each sleeve underarm seam and stitch sleeves into place, matching the shoulder seams to the centre of sleeve cast-off edge.

To attach the collar, place shorter edge of collar to the neckline with purl side of collar to WS of jacket. Beg and end 2sts in from the centre-front edge of the neck and carefully over-sew the pieces together. Fold the collar over to the RS of jacket and steam into place.

Put jacket on doll, fold fronts left over right and sew on small beads for buttons. Place belt around waist, again folding left over right, and sew on buckle or small beads as fasteners. Decorate outside edge of sleeve cuffs with 2 beads.

Stitch the inside leg seam of each trouser leg, then join the legs together in one seam from front to back. Run a gathering thread round the waist and draw up to fit.

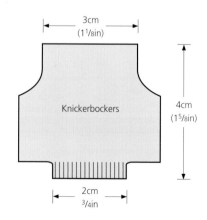

3cm
(1¹/₈in)

Knickerbockers

4cm
(1⁵/₈in)

2cm
³/₄in

Things they said
miscellaneous quotes from eminent Edwardians

'My good man, I'm not a strawberry' – Edward VII when a footman spilt cream on him

'A fully equipped Duke costs as much to keep up as two Dreadnoughts, and Dukes are just as great a terror and they last longer' – David Lloyd George

'Remember that you are an Englishman, and have consequently won first prize in the lottery of life' - Cecil Rhodes

'A man who is good enough to shed his blood for the country is good enough to be given a square deal afterwards. More than that no man is entitled to, and less than that no man shall have' – President Theodore Roosevelt

'If civilisation is to advance at all in the future, it must be through the help of women, women freed of their political shackles, women with full power to work their will in society' – Emmeline Pankhurst

'I have discovered the dance. I have discovered the art which has been lost for two thousand years' – Isadora Duncan

'Words are, of course, the most powerful drug used by mankind' – Rudyard Kipling

'The airplane stays up because it doesn't have the time to fall' – Orville Wright

'Genius is one per cent inspiration and ninety-nine per cent perspiration' – Thomas Edison

'History is more or less bunk. It's tradition. We don't want tradition. We want to live in the present, and the only history that is worth a tinker's damn is the history we make today' – Henry Ford

'Heaven, as conventionally conceived, is a place so inane, so dull, so useless, so miserable, that nobody has ever ventured to describe a whole day in heaven, though plenty of people have described a day at the seaside' – George Bernard Shaw

'God does not play dice' – Albert Einstein

'God is really only another artist. He invented the giraffe, the elephant and the cat. He has no real style. He just goes on trying other things' – Pablo Picasso

Afternoon tea

In the late afternoon it was usual for ladies to be invited to afternoon tea in the boudoir of a friend. For this ladies-only occasion a special gown was worn – loose and less structured than the day gown, and usually worn without a corset. This was a time for relaxation.

The tea gown became luxurious at-home wear, essential to gracious living, and the latest designs were illustrated

'At 5 o'clock they will don the picturesque tea-gown and adopt an air of drooping languor which savours of mystery, while striking an Oriental note of passion and colour'
The Ladies Realm, October 1901

in magazines and periodicals, along with articles on what to wear and how to wear it.

As the century progressed, men began to be admitted to these gatherings, and although it always remained an adults-only rather than a family time, this informal late afternoon, before-dinner occasion became an excuse to dispense with the corset whether indoors or out. Beautiful and elaborate tea gowns were now to be seen not just in the boudoir, but also at picnics, garden parties and other upper-class outings.

Tea for two in London in 1909, when the dress code was relaxing. Earlier in the period no Edwardian lady would have gone out to tea without hat or gloves, and her male companion would be wearing frock coat, top hat and gloves.

The gowns were high-necked, with a high waist or a yoke, and always had long sleeves. They were sumptuous and luxurious, made of silks and lace and decorated with frills, bows and ribbons. Out of doors they were always worn with gloves and an elaborate hat.

For afternoon tea the men wore a frock coat, narrow trousers and a double-breasted waistcoat. The frock coat was made from a dark material, black or grey. It was knee-length and double breasted, with straight front edges and long lapels. At the centre back the skirt had a pleat or a vent. The coat was always worn open. The straight trousers were grey or a grey-and-black narrow stripe, and the younger, very fashionable male would wear them with a centre crease. The double-breasted waistcoat usually had a shawl collar and was often made of a piqué fabric. The shirt had a high stiff collar worn with either a narrow bow tie or a cravat.

The frock coat was always accessorized with a formal top hat, gloves, a cane or walking stick and a buttonhole flower on the lapel.

FROCK COAT

The main part of the coat is knitted in one piece, beginning at the hem, working the skirt, shaping the waist, then working up to the armholes where the work is divided to complete the left front, the back, then the right front. The coat should be worn with a white shirt (half-shirt plus cuffs), and a black bow tie.

Materials
- A pair each of size 19 and size 20 needles
- Three 30m reels of Gütermann polyester top-stitching thread, in black (col 000)
- Six beads or tiny buttons
- Ribbon rose for buttonhole

Tension
8sts and 9.25 rows equal 1cm (⅜in), using size 19 needles over st st

Abbreviations
m1: make one stitch by picking up the thread that is stretched between the needles, and knitting into the back loop of it.

POCKET FLAPS
Using size 20 needles cast on 7sts, and k 1 row,
Next row: k to end,
Next row: k1, p to last st k1,
Rep the last 2 rows once more,
Leave sts on a spare needle,
Work a second flap to match.

MAIN BODY
Work coat skirt
Using size 20 needles cast on 114sts and k 1 row,
Change to size 19 needles
Next row: k43, p1, k6, p1, k12, p1, k6, p1, k to end,
Next row: k3, p to last 3sts, k3,
Rep the last 2 rows 22 times more, (a total of 46 rows)
Add pockets and work waistline
Change to size 20 needles,
Next row: k10, with the RS of pocket facing place it on the front of the work and [ktog 1 st from spare needle and 1 st from main work] 7

times, k27, cast off 26sts, k the next 26sts, then add the 7sts from the second pocket, then k to end.
Next row: k8, [k2tog, k8] to end, (80sts)
Work coat bodice
Change back to size 19 needles
1st row: k24, [k1, p1] into next st, k30, [k1, p1] into next st, k24,
2nd row: k3, p to last 3sts, k3,
3rd row: k to end,
4th row: as 2nd row
5th row: k24, [k1, p1] into next st, k32, [k1, p1] into next st, k24,
6th, 7th, 8th rows: as 2nd, 3rd, 4th rows
9th row: k24, [k1, p1] into next st, k34, [k1, p1] into next st,
10th row: k3, p to last 3, k3
Shape lapels
Next row: k3, m1, k to last 3sts, m1, k3,
Next row: k3, p to last 3sts, k3,
Next row: k3, m1, k22, [k1, p1] into next st, k36, [k1, p1] into next st, k22, m1, k3,
Next row: k3, p to last 3sts, k3,

Divide for armholes
Next row: k3, p1, m1, k18, cast off 4, k the next 39sts, cast off 4, k17, m1, p1, k3,
Work left front
Next row: k4, p17, p2tog, turn,
Cont on these 22sts only
Next row: k2tog, k16, p1, k3,
Next row: k4, p to end,
Next row: k16, p2, k3,

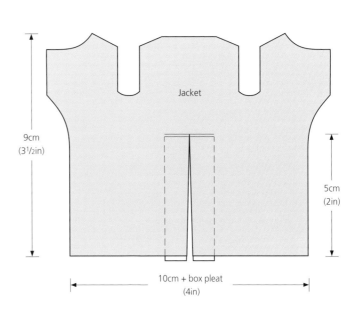

Jacket

9cm (3½in)

5cm (2in)

10cm + box pleat (4in)

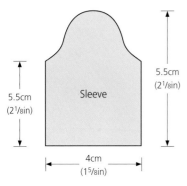

Next row: k5, p to end,
Rep last 2 rows once more,
Next row: k15, p3, k3,
Next row: k6, p to end,
Rep the last 2 rows once more,
Next row: k14, p4, k3,
Next row: k7, p to end,
Rep the last 2 rows once more,
Next row: k13, p5, k3,
Next row: k8, p to end,
Rep the last 2 rows once more
Next row: k13, p5, k3,
Shape neck
Next row: cast off 8sts, p to end,
Next row: k,
Next row: cast off 2, p the next 5sts, turn, sl1, k3, k2tog,
Cast off all 10sts.
With WS facing return to rem sts, rejoin yarn,
Next row: p2tog, p36, p2tog, turn, cont on these sts only to complete the back,
Dec 1 st at each end of the next row, then work straight for 19 rows,

Shape shoulders
Next row: k31, turn,
Next row: p6, cast off 14, p the next 5, turn,
Next row: k4, k2tog,
Cast off rem 10sts,
With RS facing return to rem sts, rejoin yarn, k2tog, k to end,
Cast off.
Work right front
Return to rem sts, with WS facing rejoin yarn,
Next row: p2tog, p17, k4,
Next row: k3, p1, p16, k2tog,
Cont to work without shaping, but match LF by working 1 extra purl st on foll 2nd row, then each foll 4th row, until 4 rows of 5 purl sts have been worked, finish with a WS row.
Shape neck
Next row: cast off 8sts, k to end,
Next row: p,
Next row: cast off 2, k the next 5, turn, sl1, p3, p2tog,.
Next row: k to end,
Cast off.

TO MAKE UP

Bag out, block and steam the pieces following the instructions in the section on finishing (page 6).

Back pleat. Fold each outer p ridge of the pleat so that WS are together, tack along the edge from hem to waist to hold the fold in place. Fold each of the inner p ridges so that RS are together and tack the edges from hem to waist. Tack the cast-off edge of the pleat to hold the inverted pleat in place and carefully steam, then slip st the folded cast off edge to the underside of back waist.

Join the shoulder seams.

Join the underarm seam of each sleeve, and stitch sleeves into place.

Place RS of the collar to the WS of the coat, matching the collar cast-off edge to the coat neckline. Beg and finish at the edge of the folded back lapel, stitching a few sts of the collar side edge to the cast-off edge of the lapel to form a 'V' shape, when collar and lapel are folded to the RS.

To each coat front add two buttons, the first one just above the waistline and about 1cm (⅜in) in from the front edge, and the second button about 1cm (⅜in) above the first.

Add two buttons about 1cm (⅜in) apart, to each side of the coat above the waistline and about 1cm (⅜in) in from the front edge. Add two buttons to centre back, side by side above the pleat.

Make a tiny ribbon rose for the left lapel.

SLEEVES

Using size 20 needles cast on 32sts and k 1 row,
Change to size 19 needles, beg with a k row, work 32 rows in st st.
Shape top
Cast off 2sts at the beg of the next 4 rows, patt 2 rows, then dec 1 st at each end of the next row, and the foll 5 RS rows, dec 1 st at each end of the next row, cast of rem 10sts.
Work a second sleeve to match.

COLLAR

Using size 20 needles, cast on 28sts, and k 1 row,
Change to size 19 needles
Next row: k to end,
Next row: k3, p to last 3sts, k3,
Rep last 2 rows once more,
Next row: k3, k2tog, k18, k2tog, k3,
Next row: k3, p to last 3sts, k3,
Next row: k to last 4sts, turn, sl1, p to last 4sts, turn,
Next row: sl1, k12, turn, sl1, k to end,
Next row: k3, p2tog, p16, p2tog, k3,
Cast off.

FORMAL TROUSERS

The trouser legs are joined together at the crotch and knitted in one piece. Note that the seam goes to the centre back. This seam is slightly shaped to accommodate the buttocks.

Materials
- A pair each of size 19 and size 20 needles
- Two 30m reels of Gütermann polyester top-stitching thread in grey (col 701)

Tension
8sts and 9.25 rows equal 1cm (⅜in), using size 19 needles over st st

RIGHT LEG

*Using size 20 needles cast on 40sts and k 1 row,
Change to size 19 needles, beg with a k row work 32 rows in st st,
Inc I st at each end of the next row, then every foll 6th row until there are 52sts, finish with a WS row*
Shape crotch
Next row: cast off 4sts, k to end,
Next row: cast off 3sts, p to last 2sts, p2tog,
Next row: K to end,

Next row: cast off 3sts, p to end,
Leave these sts on a spare needle.

LEFT LEG

Work from * to * to match R leg,
Shape crotch
Next row: cast off 3sts, k to end,
Next row: cast off 4sts, p to end,
Next row: cast off 3sts, k to last 2sts, k2tog,
Next row: p to end
Join legs
K the next row of L leg, then with RS facing cont to k across sts from spare needle (82sts)
P 1 row,
Next row: k11, turn, sl1, p to end,
Next row: k to end,
Next row: p11, turn, sl1, k to end,
Next row: p to end,
Cont in st st working straight for 16 more rows, then cast off.

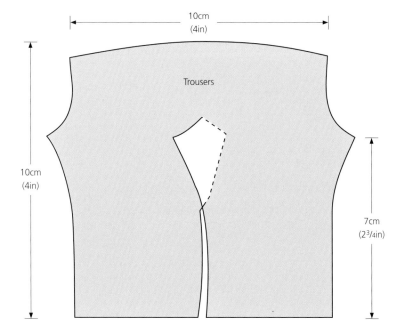

Trousers

10cm (4in)

10cm (4in)

7cm (2¾in)

TO MAKE UP

Bag out, block and steam the pieces following the instructions in the section on finishing (page 6).

Join the inside leg seam of each leg. Join the centre back and crotch seam.

Fit trousers to doll, and run a gathering thread round the waist. Draw up to fit.

DOUBLE-BREASTED WAISTCOAT

The waistcoat front is knitted in moss st to simulate a piqué fabric. The moss st fabric is reversible, so knit the R front twice, and turn one piece over to complete.

Materials
- A pair each of size 20 and size 21 needles
- 50m reel of Gütermann pure silk, S303, in white, (Col 800)
- Four small beads or buttons

Tension

8sts and 14 rows equal 1cm (⅜in), using size 20 needles over moss st

FRONT

Using size 20 needles cast on 42 sts,
Next row: [k1, p1] to end,
Next row: [p1, k1] to end,
These 2 rows form the patt and are rep throughout,
Work in patt for a total of 26 rows,
Shape cross over point
Next row: cast off 4, patt to end,
Dec 1 st at the end of the next row, and the beg of the foll row,
Work 1 row straight,
Dec 1 st at the beg of the next row, and the same edge of the foll 6th row,
Shape armhole
Cast off 2sts at beg of next row and foll alt row,
Work 2 rows straight,
Shape neck
Dec 1 st at beg of next row, and [beg of foll 6th row] 4 times, (10sts)
Work 1 row to finish at neck edge,
Next row: patt 5, turn, sl1, patt 4,
Cast off all sts.
Work second front to match.

TO MAKE UP

Bag out, block and steam the pieces following the instructions in the section on finishing (page 6).

Join shoulder seams and side seams.

Stitch the shorter of the long edges of the collar to the neckline, begin and end at the extreme outer corner of the cast-off sts of the wrap over.

Wrap the L front over the R and attach 2 buttons to each side.

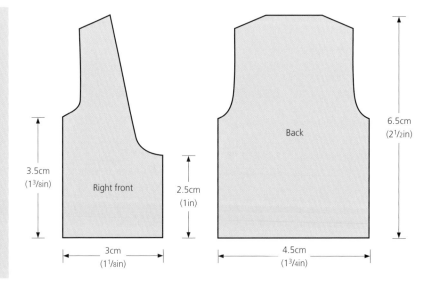

BACK

Using size 20 needles cast on 36sts and k 2 rows,
Beg with a k row, work 26 rows st st,
Shape armholes
Cast off 2 sts at the beg of the next 4 rows,
Cont in st st without shaping for 20 rows,

Shape shoulders and neck
Next row: k23, turn,
Next row: sl1, p3, cast off 10, p the next 3, turn,
Next row: sl1, k3, turn,
Cast off rem 9sts,
Return to rem sts, with RS facing rejoin yarn and k to end, then cast off.

COLLAR

Using size 21 needles cast on 1 st,
[k1, p1] into the stitch,

TEA GOWN

The gown has a lace panel down the front, which is lined with a panel of a different colour. The fan pleat fits into the centre back seam, below the folded panel. The more elaborate the decoration the better, so add lots of bows, ribbons, roses or tiny beads. Don't forget to make the matching parasol.

Materials
- A pair each of size 20 and size 21 needles
- Two 100m reels of Gütermann pure silk S303 in Lilac (col 391)
- 50m reel of Gütermann pure silk S303 in mauve (col 158)

Tension
9sts and 11 rows equal 1cm (⅜in) using size 20 needles over st st

Abbreviations
yrn, wrap the yarn round needle to make one new stitch when next stitch is a purl st

Next row: p1, [k1, p1] into next st,
Next row: [p1. k1] into next st, p1, k1
Next row: k1, p1, k1,[p1, k1] into next st
Next row: k1, p1, k1, p1, k1,
Work in moss st as now set for 25 more rows,
**Next row: patt 3, turn,
Next row: sl1, patt to end,
Work 10 rows moss st **
Rep from ** to ** 4 more times,
Next row: patt 3, turn,
Next row: sl1, patt to end,
Work in moss st without shaping for 26 rows,
Now, dec 1 st at the beg of the next row and the same edge of every row until 1 st is left, fasten off.

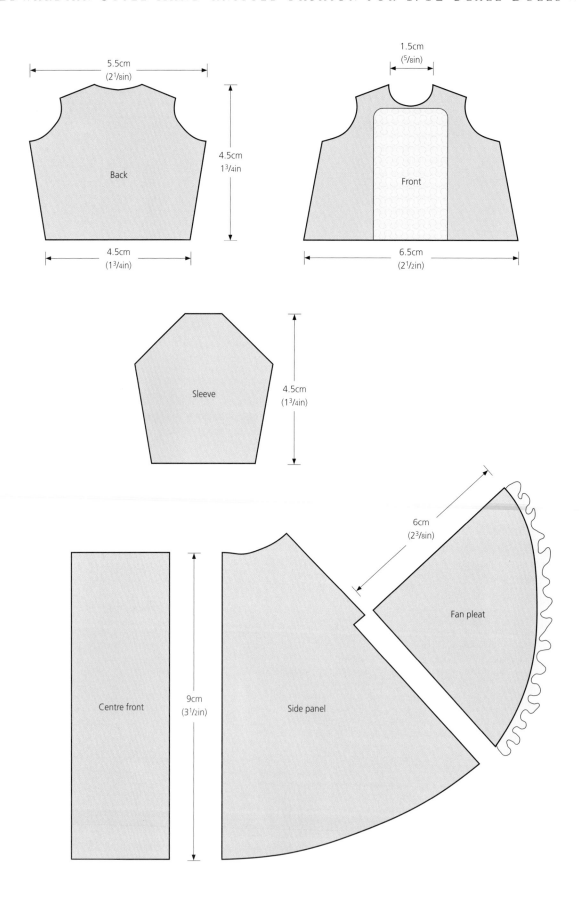

Back

5.5cm
(2¹/₈in)

4.5cm
1³/₄in

4.5cm
(1³/₄in)

1.5cm
(⁵/₈in)

Front

6.5cm
(2¹/₂in)

Sleeve

4.5cm
(1³/₄in)

Centre front

9cm
(3¹/₂in)

Side panel

Fan pleat

6cm
(2³/₈in)

2yrn, wrap yarn twice round needle to make two new stitches when next stitch is a purl stitch

yfwd-yrn, bring yarn forward then wrap round the needle to finish back in the forward position. Used to create two new sts in between two knit stitches

ssk, [slip 1 st knitwise] twice, then approaching from the left, insert the point of the LH needle into the front of these 2sts, and then knit them tog from this position

sl2tog-k1-p2sso, place the point of the RH needle into the next 2 sts as if to k2tog, do not work them, but instead, slip them both onto the RH needle, k the next st, then pass the 2 slipped sts, over the knitted st and off the needle

LACE PATTERN

Using size 20 needles and lilac, cast on 23sts and p 1 row,

1st row: k3, [yfwd, ssk, k1, k2tog, yfwd, k1], 3 times, k2,

2nd and all alt rows: p,

3rd row: k4, [yfwd, k3] 6 times, k1,

5th row: k2, k2tog, [yfwd, ssk, k1, k2tog, yfwd, sl2tog-k1-p2sso] twice, yfwd, ssk, k1, k2tog, yfwd, ssk, k2,

7th row: k2, [k1, k2tog, yfwd, k1, yfwd, ssk], 3 times, k3,

9th row: as 3rd row,

11th row: k2, [k1, k2tog, yfwd, sl2tog-k1-p2sso, yfwd, ssk] 3 times, k3,

12th row: p,

These 12 rows form the pattern and are repeated.

LACE EDGING

Using size 20 needles, cast on 3sts and p 1 row,

1st row: k1, yfwd, k2

2nd row: k4,

3rd row: k2, yfwd, k2,

4th row: k5,

5th row: k3, yfwd, k2,

6th row: k6,

7th row: k2tog, yfwd-yrn, k2, yfwd, k2,

8th row: k6, p1, k1,

9th row: k8,

10th row: cast off 5, k the next 2sts,

These 10 rows form the pattern and are repeated.

BODICE

BACK

Using size 20 needles cast on 42sts and p 1 row,

Beg with a k row work in st st and shape sides by inc 1 st at each end of the 9th row, then each end of [the foll 6th row] 3 times, (50sts),

Work 5 rows without shaping

Shape armholes

Cast off 3sts at the beg of the next 2 rows, 2sts at the beg of the next 4 rows, then dec 1 st at each end of the next row, and p 1 row,

Divide for back opening

Next row: k18, turn, k2, p to end,

Cont on these sts only to complete right neck and shoulder

Next row: k,

Next row: k2, p to end,

Rep these 2 rows once more, then k 1 row,

Shape shoulder

Next row: k2, p13, turn,
Next row: sl1, k to end,
Next row: cast off 7, p the next 4, turn,
Next row: sl1, k to end,
Cast off all 11sts.

Work left back
Return to rem sts, with RS facing rejoin yarn, cast on 2sts and k to end,
Next row: p to last 2sts, k2,
Keeping the 2 cast-on sts at centre back in garter st, work 4 rows straight,

Shape shoulder
Next row: k15, turn,
Next row: sl1, p to last 2sts, k2,
Next row: k12, turn,
Next row: sl1, p to last 2sts, k2,
Next row: cast off 7, k the next 10,
Cast off.

FRONT LACE PANEL

Follow the instructions for the Lace Pattern, work 4 repeats, cast off.

LACE PANEL TRIM

Follow the instructions for the lace edging, work 2 lengths, each 4 repeats long.

FRONT

The mauve centre panel is knitted by the intarsia Fair Isle method, using a separate length of yarn for each colour block. To prevent holes appearing twist the yarns round each other when changing colour.
Have ready 2 spools of lilac and a reel of mauve yarn.
If necessary wind a small amount of lilac yarn onto a spare spool.
Using size 20 needles and lilac yarn, cast on 60sts, and p 1 row,
Next row: lilac: k18, mauve: k24, lilac: k18,
Next row: lilac: p18, mauve: p24, lilac: p18,
Cont to work the centre panel as set.
Shape the sides by dec I st at each end of the 7th row, and then each end of [the foll 6th row] 4 times, (50sts)

Shape armholes
Cast off 3sts at the beg of the next 2 rows, and 2sts at beg of foll 4 rows,
Dec 1 st at each end of the next row,
Work 5 rows without shaping,

Change to lilac yarn,
Work 2 rows in st st,

Shape right front neck and shoulder
Next row: k14, cast off 6, k the next 10sts, turn,
Next row: sl1, p8, p2tog, turn,
Next row: k2tog, k5, turn,
Next row: sl1, p to last 2sts, p2tog, turn,
Next row: k to end, cast off.

Work left front neck and shoulder
With WS facing return to rem sts and rejoin yarn,
Next row: p2tog, p9, turn,
Next row: sl1, k to last 2sts, k2tog,
Next row: p2tog, p4, turn,
Next row: sl1, k4,
Cast off.

SLEEVES

Using size 20 needles and lilac yarn, cast on 27sts and p 1 row,
1st row: K5, [yfwd, ssk, k1, k2tog, yfwd, k1] 3 times, k4,
2nd and all alt rows: p,
3rd row: k6, [yfwd, k3] 6 times, k3,
5th row: inc into first st, k3, k2tog, [yfwd, ssk, k1, k2tog, yfwd, sl2tog-k1-p2sso] twice, yfwd, ssk, k1, k2tog, yfwd, ssk, k3, inc into next st,
7th row: k5, [k1, k2tog, yfwd, k1, yfwd, ssk] 3 times, k6,
9th row: k7, [yfwd, k3] 6 times, k4,
11th row: inc into first st, k4, [k1, k2tog, yfwd, sl2tog-k1-p2sso, yfwd, ssk] 3 times, k5, inc into last st,
13th row: K7, [yfwd, ssk, k1, k2tog, yfwd, k1] 3 times, k6,
15th row: k8, [yfwd, k3] 6 times, k5,
17th row: inc into first st, k5, k2tog, [yfwd, ssk, k1, k2tog, yfwd, sl2tog-k1-p2sso] twice, yfwd, ssk, k1, k2tog, yfwd, ssk, k5, inc into next st,
19th row: k7, [k1, k2tog, yfwd, k1, yfwd, ssk] 3 times, k8,
21st row: k9, [yfwd, k3] 6times, k6,
23rd row: inc into first st, k6, [k1, k2tog, yfwd, sl2tog-k1-p2sso, yfwd, ssk] 3 times, k7, inc into last st,
25th row: K9, [yfwd, ssk, k1, k2tog, yfwd, k1] 3 times, k8,
27th row: k10, [yfwd, k3] 6times, k7,
29th row: inc into first st, k7, k2tog, [yfwd, ssk, k1, k2tog, yfwd, sl2tog-k1-p2sso] twice, yfwd, ssk, k1, k2tog, yfwd, ssk, k7, inc into next st,

31st row: k9, [k1, k2tog, yfwd, k1, yfwd, ssk] 3 times, k10,
32nd row: p, (37sts)

Shape top
Next row: cast off 2 sts, k the next 8, [yfwd, k3] 6 times, k8,
Next row: cast off 2sts, p to end,
Next row: cast off 2sts, k the next 4, [k1, k2tog, yfwd, sl2tog-k1-p2sso, yfwd, ssk] 3 times, k to end,
Next row: cast off 2sts, p to end,

Change to plain st st, and dec 1 st at each end of the next 4 RS rows, then dec 1 st at each end of every row until 11sts remain,
Cast off.
Work a second sleeve to match.

LACE CUFFS

For each cuff work 5 repeats of the Lace Edging patt.

SHOULDER TRIM

Using size 20 needles, cast on 7sts and p 1 row,
1st row: k2, yrn, p2tog, k1, yfwd, k2
2nd row: k4, yrn, p2tog, k2,
3rd row: k2, yrn, p2tog, k2, yfwd, k2,
4th row: k5, yrn, p2tog, k2,
5th row: k2, yrn, p2tog, k3, yfwd, k2,
6th row: k6, yrn, p2tog, k2,
7th row: k2, yrn, p2tog, k2tog, yfwd-yrn, k2, yfwd, k2,
8th row: k6, p1, k1, yrn, p2tog, k2
9th row: k2, yrn, p2tog, k8,
10th row: cast off 5, k the next 2sts, yrn, p2tog, k2,
Repeat the 10 rows 5 more times, cast off.
Work a second length to match.

NECK BAND

Using size 21 needles, cast on 5sts, and p 1 row,
1st row: k1, yfwd, sl2tog-k1-p2sso, yfwd, k1,
2nd row: sl1, p3, k1,
3rd row: k1, yfwd, sl2tog-k1-p2sso, yfwd, k into fbf of next st,
4th row: cast off 2sts, p3, k1,
Rep these 4 rows, 9 times more, k1 row, then cast off.

SKIRT

FRONT LACE PANEL

Follow the instructions for the Lace Pattern, and work 8 repeats, cast off.

FRONT PANEL LINING

Using size 20 needles and mauve yarn, cast on 27sts and p 1 row,
Beg with a k row, work in st st for 100 rows,
Cast off.

FRONT PANEL LACE EDGING

Work 9 repeats of the Lace Edging pattern, which should measure 8cm (3⅛in). Check length against long edge of centre-front lace panel before casting off. You will need 2 lengths, one for each side of the centre-front skirt panel.

LEFT SIDE AND BACK PANEL

Using size 20 needles and lilac yarn, cast on 76sts and k 2 rows,
Shape hem
Next row: k to end,
Next row: p16, turn,
Next row: sl1, k to end,
Next row: p21, turn,
Next row: sl1, k to end,
Next row: p26, turn,
Next row: sl1, k to end,
Cont in this way, working an extra 5sts on each p row, until all of the sts have been worked,
Then work 2 rows with out shaping.
Shape centre back seam
Next row: k2tog, k to end,
Next row: p to end,
Next row: k2tog, k to end,
Next row: p to last 2sts, p2tog,
1st row: k to end,
2nd row: p to last 2sts, p2tog,
3rd row: k2tog, k to end,
4th row: p to end,
5th row: k2tog, k to end,
6th row: p to last 2sts, p2tog,
Repeat the last 6 rows, until there are 45sts,
Next row: cast on 4sts, k to end,

Now, at the same edge as before dec 1 st on every row, until there are 25sts,
Shape waistline
Next row: (WS) cast off 9sts, p to last 2, p2tog,
Dec 1 st at each end of every row until there are 3sts,
Cast off.

RIGHT SIDE AND BACK PANEL

Using size 20 needles and lilac yarn, cast on 76sts and k 2 rows,
Shape hem
Next row: k16, turn,
Next row: sl1, p to end,
Next row: k21, turn,
Next row: sl1, p to end,
Next row: k26, turn,
Next row: sl1, p to end,
Cont in this way working 5 extra sts on each k row until all the sts have been worked,
Work 3 rows straight,
Shape centre back seam
Next row: k to last 2sts, k2tog,
Next row: p to end,
Next row: k to last 2sts, k2tog,
Next row: p2tog, p to end,
Next row: k to end,
1st row: p2tog, p to end,
2nd row: k to last 2sts, k2tog,
3rd row: p to end,
4th row: k to last 2sts, k2tog,
5th row: p2tog, p to end,
6th row: k to end,
Repeat the last 6 rows until there are 45sts left,
Next row: cast on 4sts, p to end, Now at the same edge as before, dec 1 st on every row until there are 25sts,
Shape waistline
Next row: cast off 9sts, k to end,
Dec 1 st at each end of every row until 3sts are left,
Cast off.

HEM EDGING

Work 21 repeats of the Lace Edging pattern.

BACK FAN PLEAT

Using size 20 needles and lilac yarn, cast on 45sts,

1st row: k40, yrn, p2tog, k1, yfwd, k2,
2nd row: k4, yrn, p2tog, p36, turn,
3rd row: sl1, k35, yrn, p2tog, k2, yfwd, k2,
4th row: k5, yrn, p2tog, p32, turn,
5th row: sl1, k31, yrn, p2tog, k3, yfwd, k2,
6th row: k6, yrn, p2tog, p28, turn,
7th row: sl1, k27, yrn, p2tog, k2tog, yfwd, yrn, k2, yfwd, k2,
8th row: k5, [k1, p1] into the double wrap of previous row, k1, yrn, p2tog, p24, turn,
9th row: sl1, k23, yrn, p2tog, k8,
10th row: cast off 5, k the next 2sts, yrn, p2tog, p20, turn,
11th row: sl1, k19, yrn, p2tog, k1, yfwd, k2,
12th row: k4, yrn, p2tog, p16, turn,
13th row: sl1, k15, yrn, p2tog, k2, yfwd, k2,
14th row: k5, yrn, p2tog, p12, turn,
15th row: sl1, k11, yrn, p2tog, k3, yfwd, k2,
16th row: k6, yrn, p2tog, p8, turn,
17th row: sl1, k7, yrn, p2tog, k2tog, yfwd, yrn, k2, yfwd, k2,
18th row: k5, [k1, p1] into the double wrap of previous row, k1, yrn, p2tog, p4, turn,
19th row: sl1, k3, yrn, p2tog, k8,
20th row: cast off 5, k the next 2sts, yrn, p2tog, p2, [yrn, p2tog] to last 2sts, p2,
Rep the last 20 row patt 7 more times,
Cast off.

SMALL BACK FOLD

Using size 20 needles and lilac yarn, cast on 14sts and k 3 rows,
Next row: k fbf, into each st, (42sts)
Beg with a k row, work 32 rows in st st
Mark fold line
k the next 2 rows,
Beg with a k row work 32 rows in st st
Next row: [k3tog] to end,
k 3 rows, cast off.

LONG BACK FOLD

Using size 20 needles, cast on 15sts, and k 3 rows,
Next row: k into fbf of each st, (45sts)
Work 56 rows in st st,
Mark fold line
k the next 2 rows,
Beg with a k row work 56 rows st st,
Next row: [p3tog] to end, (15sts),
K 3 rows,
Cast off.

TO MAKE UP

Bag out, block and steam the pieces following the instructions in the section on finishing (page 6).

Skirt. Stitch the front lining panel into the skirt by matching each long edge of panel to the straight edges of the skirt, side and back panel. Make sure that right sides are together, and stitch seam with a tiny backstitch. The lining is now in the centre of the 2 skirt pieces.

Place the skirt lace panel on top of the lining, and top stitch into place. Slip-stitch a length of lace trim down each long edge of the lace. Join the centre-back seam of the skirt, from the waist to the 4 cast on sts. Stitch the fan pleat into the open lower section.

Back folds. For each fold, fold on the marked line and with RS together stitch the two edges together to form a bag. Turn RS out and stitch the narrow edge of the small fold to the centre-back waistline of the skirt. The top edge of the large fold is stitched to the skirt just below the waistline, underneath the top fold.

Place the skirt on the doll and run a gathering thread round the waistline, draw up to fit. Arrange the gathers so that most are at the back, leaving the front flat.

Bodice. Join the side seams of the bodice. Place the lace panel on top of the lining. Stitch into place. Stitch a length of lace trim to each side edge of the panel.

Join the shoulder seams.

Beginning and ending at the centre back, stitch the straight edge of the collar to the neckline so that it stands up as a band round the neck. At the base of the back opening, secure the under-wrap cast-on sts to the under side of bodice.

Stitch a length of cuff lace to the cast-on edge of each sleeve and join the underarm seam. Stitch sleeves into place.

Beg and end about 0.5cm (³⁄₁₆in) from the underarm seam. Carefully stitch a length of lace trim to the armhole-sleeve seam, gathering it slightly at the shoulder point.

Put the bodice on the doll and stitch up the centre-back opening. Run a gathering thread round the waistline and draw up to fit.

Decorate the gown with a silk ribbon belt. Add bows and ribbons as preferred.

PARASOL

Materials
- A pair of size 20 needles
- 50m reel of Gütermann pure silk S303, in mauve (col 158)
- A cocktail stick or something similar, like a length of fine brass tubing
- Tiny beads, narrow ribbon, and small bows for decoration

Tension
9sts and 11 rows equal 1cm (⅜in) using size 20 needles over st st

Using size 20 needles and lilac yarn, cast on 45sts,
1st row: k40, yrn, p2tog, k1, yfwd, k2,
2nd row: k4, yrn, p2tog, p36, turn,
3rd row: sl1, k35, yrn, p2tog, k2, yfwd, k2,
4th row: k5, yrn, p2tog, p32, turn,
5th row: sl1, k31, yrn, p2tog, k3, yfwd, k2,
6th row: k6, yrn, p2tog, p28, turn,
7th row: sl1, k27, yrn, p2tog, k2tog, yfwd-yrn, k2, yfwd, k2,
8th row: k6, p1, k1, yrn, p2tog, p24, turn,
9th row: sl1, k23, yrn, p2tog, k8,
10th row: cast off 5, k the next 2sts, yrn, p2tog, p20, turn,
11th row: sl1, k19, yrn, p2tog, k1, yfwd, k2,
12th row: k4, yrn, p2tog, p16, turn,

TO MAKE UP

Block and steam the piece of knitting, following the instructions in the section on finishing (page 6).

Join the seam from the point to the cast-on edge to form a cone shape.

Insert a cocktail stick or something similar through the hole at the pointed end of the knitted cone. Use a needle and thread to gather the knit to fit, and add a spot of glue.

Gently pull the full end of the knit up the stick and run a gathering thread just below the lace edge. Pull up to fit, gently swirl the parasol round the stick to make folds and add a spot of glue.

Decorate the handle with beads and streamers or bows.

13th row: sl1, k15, yrn, p2tog, k2, yfwd, k2,
14th row: k5, yrn, p2tog, p12, turn,
15th row: sl1, k11, yrn, p2tog, k3, yfwd, k2,
16th row: k6, yrn, p2tog, p8, turn,
17th row: sl1, k7, yrn, p2tog, k2tog, yfwd-yrn, k2, yfwd, k2,
18th row: k6, p1, k1, yrn, p2tog, p4, turn,
19th row: sl1, k3, yrn, p2tog, k8,
20th row: cast off 5, k the next 2sts, yrn, p2tog, p2, [yrn, p2tog] to last 2sts, p2,
Repeat these 20 rows 3 more times,
Cast off.

The Edwardian Age
art & fashion

1901

Pablo Picasso's first exhibition, in Paris

Kodak founder George Eastman sets up international camera company

Gillette announces marketing of replaceable razor

1902

First special effects film made, in Paris

Kipling's *Just So Stories* and Beatrix Potter's *Tale of Peter Rabbit* published

1903

'The Wonderful Wizard of Oz' opens on Broadway

The Great Train Robbery is first shown in America

1904

Tenor Enrico Caruso makes his first American recording

Roller skating becomes a popular pastime

J.M. Barrie's 'Peter Pan' opens to great acclaim in London

1905

Conan Doyle, bowing to public demand, brings back his famous hero in *The Return of Sherlock Holmes*

'Les Fauves' (including Matisse and Braque) stage a revolutionary exhibition in Paris

Bernard Shaw's *Man and Superman* and *Major Barbara* premiered in London

1906

John Galsworthy launches his *Forsyte Saga* with *A Man of Property*

Invention of the triode valve enables production of more powerful wireless transmitters

1907

Picasso's 'Les Damoiselles d'Auvignon' establishes Cubist art

Rudyard Kipling awarded the Nobel Prize for Literature

J.M. Synge's *The Playboy of the Western World* is first staged

1908

Sir Edward Elgar writes his first symphony

Kenneth Grahame's *The Wind in the Willows* is published

The liberty bodice is introduced

1909

Colour films are screened for the first time, at Brighton, Sussex

Saucy postcards are all the rage at the seaside

The Ballet Russes ballet is a sensation in Paris

H.G. Wells publishes *Tono-Bungay*

1910

Kandinsky champions abstract art

Stravinsky causes a sensation with his score for 'The Firebird'

A day at the seaside

Clothing for leisure, holidays and travel became a little more relaxed at the turn of the century, but Edwardian ladies still had to be covered from head to foot – even on the beach. For bathing, a knee-length dress with a collar and short sleeves was worn with pantalets to the knee or ankle, always in sombre colours and with excessive

'The Victorians had not been anxious to go away for the weekend. The Edwardians, on the contrary, were nomadic'

T.H. White: 'Farewell Victoria'

Bank Holiday crowds at Southend, Essex – popularly known to the Edwardians as 'East London on Sea'

decoration, designs based on the sailor suit being most popular. This dress was often worn over the corset. Black stockings plus tie-on shoes were obligatory, and a hat (often quite elegant or elaborate) was always worn. Towards the end of the period lighter colours were introduced and became very popular, but it was not until around 1914 that the one-piece bathing costume made its appearance.

Until about 1850 it was usual for men to bathe nude on special men-only beaches, but by 1880 the all-in-one bathing costume was worn. This covered the body from shoulders to mid-thigh and was often made from a striped knitted jersey fabric. The elastic quality of knitted jersey was a great improvement on previous fabrics, being lighter in weight and more comfortable to wear, and giving a better fit, too.

The summer blazer worn with light-weight flannels was popular for casual wear. The blazer was often light and bright in colour, and usually had a vertical stripe.

For children the new woollen jerseys were becoming increasingly popular for holiday, outdoor and sporting dress. Many magazines now published knitting patterns for the home knitter to produce her own. However the ubiquitous sailor suit, worn with black stockings and shoes, was still the preferred beach garment for both girls and boys.

LADY'S BATHING COSTUME

The bodice of this bathing dress has a striped yoke. This is knitted by the intarsia method, with a separate length of yarn used for each colour. The yarns are not stranded across the back of the work.

Materials:
- A pair of size 20 needles
- Two 100m reels of Gütermann pure silk S303, in main colour (M) navy (col 339)
- A small amount of Gütermann pure silk in contrast colour (C1) red (col 46)
- A small amount of Gütermann pure silk, in contrast colour (C2) cream (col 802)
- Very fine 'knitting in' elastic
- Two tiny beads, for buttons

Tension:
9sts and 11 rows equal 1 cm (⅜in), using size 20 needles over st st

Abbreviations:
M: Main yarn, navy, **C1**: first contrast yarn, red
C2: second contrast yarn, cream
k-f b: knit into the front then the back of next st
p-f b: p into the front then back of next st
p-f b f: purl into the front, then back, then front again of the next st.

PANTALOONS

Using size 20 needles and M, cast on 71sts
Change to C1, and k2 rows,
Change to M and work patt as folls,
1st row: k4, *sl1-k2tog-psso, k7, rep from *, but end last rep k4 instead of k7,
2nd row: p-f b, p7, * p-f b f , p7 rep from * to last st, p-f b,
Rep the last 2 rows once more, then cont in st st for 6 rows,
Next row: [k1, k2tog] 7 times, [k2, k2tog] 7 times, [k1, k2tog] 7 times, k1, (50sts)
Next row: p,
Cont in st st but inc 1 st at each end of the foll 11th row, then each end of [the foll 4th row] 4 times, then the next 4 alt rows, finish with a WS row, (68sts)
Shape crotch

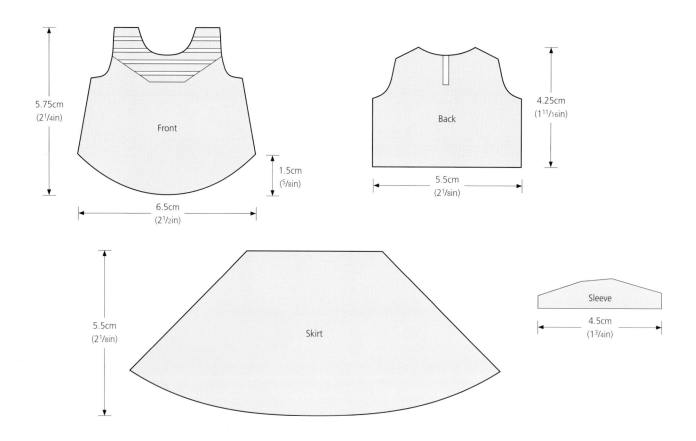

Cast off 3sts at the beg of the next 4 rows, then dec 1 st. at each end of the next row, and the foll 2 alt rows, finish with a WS row, Leave these 50sts on a spare needle, and work a second leg to match.

Join legs

With RS of both legs facing, knit 1 row across second leg sts, then cont to knit across the sts from the spare needle, (100sts)

Work in st st for 19 more rows, then cast off.

BATHING DRESS

SKIRT

Using size 20 needles and M yarn, cast on 50sts

1st row: p2, [k2, p2,] to end,
2nd row: k2, [p2, k2,] to end,
rep these 2 rows twice more,
7th row: p2, [k-f b, k1, p2,] to end,
8th row: k2, [p3, k2] to end,
Cont in rib without shaping for 4 more rows,
13th row: p2, [k-f b, k2, p2] to end,
14th row: k2, [p4, k2] to end,

Cont in rib without shaping for 4 more rows,
19th row: p2, [k-f b, k3, p2] to end,
20th row: k2, [p5, k2] to end,
Cont to increase in this way, on each foll 6th row, until you have completed the k2, p11, k2, row (158sts), follow this with 4 rows of the rib patt then change to C1 yarn and using a size larger needle cast off loosely.

BODICE BACK

Using size 20 needles and navy yarn cast on 50sts, and work 30 rows in st st

Shape armholes

Cast off 3sts at the beg of the next 2 rows, 2sts at the beg of the foll 4 rows,

Next row: k2tog, k17, turn, cont on these sts only, to complete the R back,

Next row: k2, p to end,

Keeping the 2 centre sts in g st as set, cont in st st for 6 more rows without shaping,

Shape shoulders and neck

Cast off 3sts at the beg of next row and foll alt row.

Next row: WS facing, cast off 9sts, k to end,
Cast off rem 3sts.
With RS facing, return to rem sts, cast on 2sts, and k to last 2sts, k2tog,
Next row: p to last 2sts, k2,
Cont in st st as now set, and work 7 more rows, without shaping.
Cast off 3sts at the beg of the next row and the foll alt row,
Next row: cast off 9sts, k to end.
Cast off rem 3sts.

BODICE FRONT

Using size 20 needles and navy (M) yarn, cast on 60sts, and k 2 rows,
Next row: k57, turn,
Next row: sl1, p53, turn,
Next row: sl1, k50, turn,
Next row: sl1, p47, turn,
Cont in this way working 3sts less on each row, until you have worked the sl1, p17 row, now turn and k to end,
then p 1 row,
Cont in st st but at the same time dec 1 st at each end of the next row, then [every foll 6th row] 4 times, finish with a WS row, (50sts)

Shape armholes and yoke
1st row: M: cast off 3sts, k16, C1: k10, M; k to end,
2nd row: M: cast off 3sts, p16, C1: k10, M: p to end,
3rd row: M: cast off 2sts, k12, C2: k14, M: k to end,
4th row: M: cast off 2sts, p12, C2: p14, M: p to end,
5th row: M: cast off 2sts, k8, C1: k18, M: k to end,
6th row: cast off 2sts, M: p8, C1: k18, M: p to end,
7th row: M: k2tog, k5, C2: k22, M: k to last 2sts, k2tog,
8th row: M: p6, C2: p22, M: p to end,
9th row: M: k4, C1: k26, M: k to end,
10th row: M: p4, C1: k26, M: p to end,
11th row: M: k2, C2: k30, M: k2,
12th row: M: p2, C2: k30, M: p2,
13th row: C1: k12, cast off 10, k to end,
14th row: C1: k10, k2tog, turn,
Cont on these sts only, to complete R shoulder,
Next row: C2: k2tog, k to end,
Next row: C2: p to last 2sts, p2tog
Next 2 rows: C1: k,

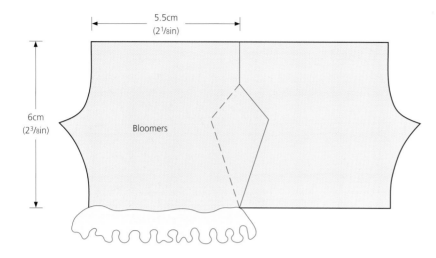

Bloomers

5.5cm
(2¹/₈in)

6cm
(2³/₈in)

Next row: C2: k,
Cast off.
With WS facing return to the rem sts, rejoin C1,
k2tog, and k to end,
Next row: C2: k to last 2sts, k2tog,
Next row: C2: p2tog, p to end,
Next 2 rows: C1: k,
Next row: C2: k,
Cast off.

SLEEVES

Using size 20 needles and navy (M) yarn, cast on
41sts, and k 1 row,
**Change to C1, and k2 rows,
Change to M and work patt as folls,
1st row: k4, *sl1-k2tog-psso, k7, rep from *,
but end last rep k4 instead of k7,
2nd row: p-f b, p7, * p-f bf, p7 rep from * to
last st, p-f b,
Rep the last 2 rows once more,** then cont with
M yarn and st.st, and cast off 5sts at the beg of
the next 6 rows, then cast off rem 11sts.
Work a second sleeve to match.

NECK BAND

Using size 20 needles and C1, cast on 36sts,
then cast them off, fairly tightly.

BOW DECORATION

Using size 20 needles and C1, cast on about
70sts, then cast them off again.

BATHING CAP

Using size 20 needles and M yarn, cast on
121sts, and K 1 row,
Work from ** to ** to match sleeves, Cont in M
yarn,
Work eyelets
Next row: [k2tog, yfwd], to last 3sts, k2tog, k1,
(120sts),
Next row: p to end,
Shape crown
1st row: [k2tog, k10] to end,
Next and all WS rows: p,
3rd row: [k2tog, k9] to end,
5th row: [k2tog, k8] to end ,
Cont in this way reducing the sts, when there are
10sts left, break off yarn, and thread the end
through the rem sts and fasten off.

TO MAKE UP

Bag out, block and steam the pieces following the instructions in the
section on finishing (page 6).

Pantaloons. Join the inside leg seams, then the centre back and crotch
seam.

Run a gathering thread round the waistline and draw up to fit.

Dress. Join the bodice side and shoulder seams.

Join the underarm seam on each sleeve, and stitch the sleeves into
place. Beginning and ending at the centre-back, stitch the cast-on edge
of the neck-band to the neck line.

Join the centre-back seam of the skirt, then matching both centre-back
seams join the skirt to the bodice, gathering to fit. Put the dress on the
doll, stitch up the bodice back opening. Run a gathering thread of fine
knitting-in elastic or silk sewing thread through the waistline, and then
pull up to fit, blousing the front of the bodice. It should drape over the
skirt waistline.

Add bow decoration to neckline.

Bathing cap. Join the seam to form a circle, run an elastic thread
through the eyelet holes and draw up to fit.

MALE BATHING COSTUME

The main body of this swimming costume is knitted in one piece with a seam at the centre-back. The shaping at the hip and waist is achieved by using different sized needles. In order to get the right look, it is necessary for the costume to fit very closely. This may mean that you have to leave the top of the back seam open, finishing the stitching after dressing your doll.

Materials:
- A pair each of size 22, size 21 and size 20 needles
- 100m reel of Gütermann pure silk S303, in cream (col 802)
- 50m reel of Gütermann pure silk S303, in red (col 46)

Tension:
9sts and 11 rows equal 1 cm (⅜in), using size 20 needles over st st

Abbreviations:
m1, make one stitch, pick up the thread that is stretched between the needles, and knit into the back loop of it.

STRIPE PATTERN

1st row: using cream yarn, k,
2nd row: using cream yarn, p,
3rd row: using red yarn, k,
4th row: using red yarn, p,
These 4 rows form the patt and are used throughout.

MAIN BODY

Work first leg
Using size 21 needles and cream yarn cast on 36sts, and work 4 rows in 1x1 rib,
Change to size 20 needles and stripe patt inc 1st at each end of the next row, then [each end of every foll 4th row] 6 times, (50sts)
Patt 1 row
Shape crotch
Cast off 4sts at the beg of the next 4 rows, leave these 34 sts on a spare needle.
Knit a second leg to match.

Join legs

Make sure that RS of each piece is facing you, then patt across the second leg, and cont across the sts from spare needle, (68sts)
Patt 19 rows without shaping.

Shape waist

Change to size 21 needles, patt 4 rows,
Change to size 22 needles, patt 8 rows,
Change to size 21 needles, patt 4 rows,
Change to size 20 needles,
Next row: patt 16, m1, patt2, m1, patt32, m1, patt2, m1, patt to end,
Next row: patt to end,
Next row: patt 17, m1, patt 2, m1, patt 34, m1, patt 2, m1, patt to end,
Next row: patt to end,

Divide for armholes

Next row: patt 17, cast off 4, patt next 33, cast off 4, patt to end.

Work right back

Next row: patt 17 turn, cont on these 17 sts only to complete the R back,
**Cast off 2sts at the beg of next row, then dec 1st at the beg of foll alt row, (14sts)
Patt 10 rows straight,

Shape neck

Cast off 4sts at beg of next row, and 2sts at beg of foll alt row,
Patt 4 rows to finish at armhole edge,
Cast off 4sts at beg of next row and foll alt row**

Work front

With WS facing rejoin yarn to rem sts,
Patt 34sts and turn, cont on these 34sts only, working in patt for 12 more rows,

Shape neck

Next row: patt 12, cast off 10, patt to end,
Next row: patt 12, turn, cont on these 12sts only, and cast off 2sts at beg of next row and foll alt row, then patt straight for 4 rows to finish at armhole edge,

Shape shoulder

Cast off 4sts at beg of next row and foll alt row.
With WS facing return to rem 12sts of the front, rejoin yarn and patt 2 rows,
Cast off 2sts at the beg of the next row and foll alt row, patt 4 rows to finish at armhole edge,

Shape shoulder

Cast off 4sts at beg of next row and foll alt row.

Work the left back

With the WS facing return to the rem sts, rejoin yarn, and work from ** to ** to match R back.

SLEEVES

Using size 21 needles and cream yarn, cast on
26sts and work 4 rows in 1x1 rib,
Change to size 20 needles and stripe patt
Inc 1 st at each end of the next row, then [every
foll 4th row] 3 times,
Patt 3 rows straight.

Shape top

Cast off 2sts at beg of next 4 rows,
Dec 1 st at each end of the next row, and [each
end of every foll alt row] twice,
patt 1 row,
Dec 1 st at each end of the next 6 rows and cast
off rem 8sts.
Work a second sleeve to match.

NECK TRIM

Using size 21 needles cast on 64sts, work in 1x1
rib for 3 rows, then cast off quite tightly in rib.
(The rib band needs to be curved so make sure
that the cast off edge is slightly tighter than the
cast on edge.)

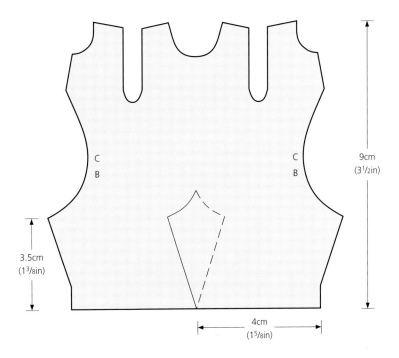

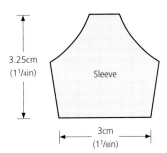

TO MAKE UP

Bag out, block and steam the pieces following the instructions in the
chapter on finishing (page 6).

Join each leg seam, then join the crotch and centre-back seam leaving
about 2cm (¾in) open at the neck edge. Join the shoulder seams. Stitch
the cast on edge of the neck trim to the neck edge.

Join sleeve seams, and stitch sleeves into place. Give a final gentle steam
to all seams and the neck line.

Fit to doll, and either complete the back seam or add a bead button and
a buttonholed loop.

BLAZER AND FLANNELS

The blazer is knitted sideways, with the purl side as the right side. The main body is knitted in one piece, beginning with the left front buttonhole band and finishing with the right front button edge.

Materials
Blazer
- A pair of size 19 needles
- Two 30m reels of Gütermann top stitch thread, 100% polyester, in pale grey (col 8)
- Reel of Gütermann top stitch thread 100% polyester, in navy (col 232)

Trousers
- A pair each of size 20 and size 21 needles
- 100m reel of Gütermann pure silk S303, in pale grey (col 8),

Tension
8sts and 9 rows equal 1cm (⅜in), using size 19 needles and polyester, over the blazer stripe pattern.
9sts and 11 rows equal 1cm (⅜in), using size 20 needles and silk, over st st

Abbreviations
yrn, wrap yarn round needle to make one new stitch

STRIPE PATTERN

(**note:** the purl side is the right side)
In order to avoid a hole, twist the yarns round each other when changing colour
1st row: grey: k2, navy: p to end
2nd row: navy: k to last 2sts, grey: k2,
3rd row: grey: p
4th row: grey: k
These 4 rows form the pattern and are used throughout.

BLAZER

Begin at left front
Using size 19 needles and grey thread cast on 38sts, and k 2 rows
Next row: p5, yrn, p2tog, [p6, yrn, p2tog,] twice, k to end,
Next row: p12, k to last st, inc into last st.

Now join in the navy thread and begin to work in the stripe patt.

Note that the centre-front curve is worked by shaping inside the grey border on the hem edge.

1st row: grey: k2, navy: inc into next st, p 27, k to end,

2nd row: navy: p9, k to last 3sts, inc into next st, grey: k2,

3rd row: grey: k2, inc into next st. p 32, k to end,

4th row: grey: p6, k to end,

5th row: grey: k2, inc into next st, p 36, k to end,

Shape left front neck

6th row: grey: inc into first st, p2, k to end.

Working all hem edge shaping 2sts in as before, and keeping stripe pattern correct cont as folls.

Inc 1 st at each end of the next row, patt 1 row,

Inc 1 st at the beg of the next row,

Patt 1 row

Shape left front shoulder

Next row: inc into 3rd st patt to last 2sts, p2tog,

** Patt 3 rows, then dec 1 st. at the end of the next row, patt 2 rows,

Shape armhole

Cast off 16sts at the beg of next row, patt 1 row,

Dec 1 st at the armhole edge of the next 4 rows, (26 sts)

Work 5 rows straight.

Inc 1 st at the armhole edge of the next 4 rows,

Patt 1 row to finish at armhole edge,

Next row: cast on 16sts, patt to end,

then patt 2 rows straight. (46sts)***

Shape left back shoulder

Inc 1 st at the end of the next row, and the foll 4th row, then patt 3 rows straight,

Shape back neck

Dec 1 st at the neck edge of the next 2 rows, then patt 13 rows without shaping, to finish at the neck edge,

Inc 1 st at the neck edge of the next 2 rows, patt 3 rows straight,

Shape right back shoulder

Dec 1 st at the end of the next row, then foll instructions from ** to ***

Shape right front shoulder

Inc 1 st at the end of next row, then patt 3 rows,

Next row: k2, p2tog, p to last st, inc into last st,

Next row: patt to end,

Next row: k2, p2tog, p to end,

Next row: patt to end

Next row: k2, p2tog, p37, k3, k2tog,

Next row: p2tog, p2, k to end,

Next row: k2, p2tog, p33, k6,

Next row: p6, k to end,

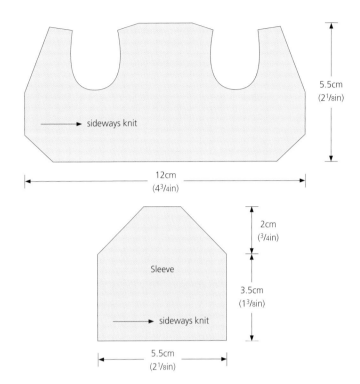

sideways knit

5.5cm (2¹⁄₈in)

12cm (4³⁄₄in)

2cm (³⁄₄in)

Sleeve

3.5cm (1³⁄₈in)

sideways knit

5.5cm (2¹⁄₈in)

Next row: k2, p2tog, p29, k9,

Next row: p9, k to last 4sts, k2tog, k2,

Next row: k2, p2tog, p24, k12,

Next row: p12, k to last 4sts, k2tog, k2.

Using grey thread cast off loosely.

SLEEVES

Using size 19 needles and grey thread cast on 29sts and p 1 row,

Next row: k8, turn, sl1, p6, inc into next st,

Next row: inc into first st, k17, turn, sl1, p to last st inc into last st,

Next row: inc into first st, k to end,

Join in navy thread and working in stripe pattern, inc 1 st at the end of the next row,

Cast on 2sts at the beg of the next row, and [the foll alt row] 3 times, then patt 1 row,

Inc 1 st at beg of next row, and the same edge of foll 3 rows, then patt 13 rows without shaping,

Dec 1 st at the end of the next row, then the same edge of foll 3 rows,

patt 1 row,

Cast off 2sts at the beg of the next row, and [the foll alt row] 3 times,

Break off navy thread and cont with grey thread only,

Dec 1 st at the end of the next row,

Next row: K2tog, k17, turn, sl1, p15, k2tog,

Next row: k2tog, k7, turn, sl1, p5, p2tog,

Next row: k across all sts,
Cast off.
Work a second sleeve to match.

COLLAR

Using size 19 needles and grey thread, cast on 4sts,
Join in navy thread and work in stripe pattern,
1st row: p,
2nd row: inc into first st, k to end,
3rd row: p to last st, inc into last st,
4th row: k to last 3sts, inc into next st, k2,
5th row: p,
6th row: k to last 3sts, inc into next st, k2,
Patt 2 rows straight,
Next row: patt 5, turn, sl1, patt to end,
Cont in stripe patt working 12 rows without shaping,
Next row: patt 5, turn, sl1, patt to end,

Patt 3 rows,
Next row: patt to last 4sts, k2tog, k2,
Next row: patt to end,
Next row: patt to last 4sts, k2tog, k2,
Next row: patt to last 2sts, p2tog,
Next row: k2tog, patt to end,
Using grey thread cast off.

POCKET

Using size 19 needles and grey thread,
cast on 8sts,
Join in navy thread and working in stripe pattern,
patt 1 row,
Inc 1 st at beg of next row, then work 5 rows straight,
Dec 1 st at beg of next row, then using grey thread, Cast off.
Work two more pockets to match.

FLANNEL TROUSERS

Using size 21 needles and silk thread cast on 50 sts, and k 1 row,
Change to size 20 needles, beg with a k row and work 50 rows in st st,
Shape leg
Inc 1 st. at each end of the next row, and each end of the [foll 8th row] 3 times, then work 5 rows straight, (58sts)
Shape crotch
Cast off 3sts at the beg of the next 4 rows, then cont in st st for a further 26 rows,
Cast off.
Work a second leg to match.

TO MAKE UP

Bag out, block and steam the pieces following the instructions in the chapter on finishing (page 6).

Blazer. On the front of the blazer fold back the top centre front corners so that the purl side of each corner is to the front and forms the lapel part of the collar. Give them a little steam and use your fingers to reinforce the fold.
Join shoulder seams. Join sleeve underarm seam. Starting and ending about 1cm (⅜in) away from seam, run a gathering around the sleeve head. Pull up just enough to give a slightly dished shape to the top, but prevent any gathers showing. Match the centre of the sleeve head to the shoulder seam and carefully stitch into place.

Attach the pockets by placing on the jacket and matching the stripes. The two lower ones need to be about 0.5cm (³⁄₁₆in) from the bottom edge, and the top of the breast pocket about level with the start of the revere collar. Stitch on using a small hemming stitch.

Make sure that the grey edging of the collar is at the outside edge. Stitch the other long edge to the neck, matching the shaped edge of the first and last navy stripes of the collar to the first navy stripes at each centre-front edge of the blazer.

Trousers. Join each leg seam. Placing RS together and matching the leg seams, join the centre-front, crotch and back seam. Run a length of fine elastic through the waist and draw up to fit.

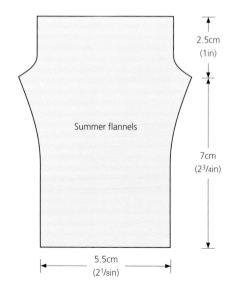

Summer flannels

2.5cm (1in)

7cm (2³⁄₄in)

5.5cm (2¹⁄₈in)

GIRL'S SAILOR SUIT

This sailor suit is in fact a one-piece dress worn over matching bloomers. The top of the dress is bloused in typical Edwardian style, and the skirt is pleated.

Materials
- A pair each of size 20 and size 21 needles
- 50m reel of Gütermann pure silk, S303, in cream (col 802)
- 50m reel of Gütermann pure silk, S303, in navy blue (col 339)
- Short length of fine knitting-in elastic
- Ribbon bow, or some red sewing thread or silk for knitted bow

Tension
9sts and 11 rows equal 1cm (⅜in) using size 20 needles over st st

BACK
Begin at the skirt hem,
Using size 21 needles and navy yarn, cast on 64sts
1st row: [k6, p2] to end,
2nd row: [k2, p6,] to end,
Change to size 20 needles, and rep the last 2 rows, 4 times more,
11th row: [k4, k2tog, p2] to end,
12th row: [k2, p5] to end,
13th row: [k5, p2] to end,
14th row: [k2, p5] to end,
Rep the last 2 rows, 3 times more
21st row: [k3, k2tog, p2] to end,
22nd row: [k2, p4] to end,
Cont in rib patt as now set, dec as before on the foll 8th row, then each foll 10th row, until the WS row, [k2, p2] has been knitted, (32sts)
Work bodice
Change to cream yarn, beg with a k row and work 10 rows in st st,
Work stripes
Next 2 rows: navy yarn, st st,
Next 2 rows: cream yarn, st st,
Next 2 rows: navy yarn, st st
Cont in cream yarn for 6 more rows,
Shape armholes
Cast off 2sts at the beg of the next 2 rows,
Dec 1 st at each end of the next 2 rows**

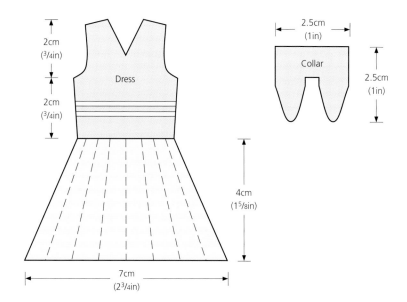

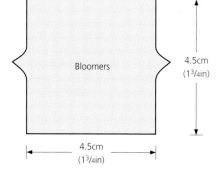

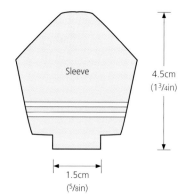

Work straight for 15 rows, to finish with a RS row,
Shape shoulders
Next row: p20, turn,
Next row: sl1, k15, turn,
Next row: sl1, p to end,
Cast off.

FRONT

Foll instructions for the back until ** is reached,
Work straight for 4 more rows,
Shape neck
Next row: patt 12, turn,
cont on these sts only to complete the left side of front,
Next row: p2tog, p to end,
Dec 1 st at the neck edge of the foll 3rd row, then the same edge of the foll 4th row, patt 2 rows,
Shape shoulder
Next row: p5, turn,
Next row: sl1, k2, k2tog,
Next row: p to end
Cast off.
Return to rem sts, with RS facing rejoin yarn and patt to end,
Next row: p to last 2 sts, p2tog,
Dec 1 st at the neck edge of the foll 3rd row, then the same edge of the foll 4th row, patt 3 rows,
Shape shoulder
Next row: k2tog, k3, turn,
Next row: p4,
Cast off

SLEEVES

Using size 21 needles and navy yarn cast on 14sts, and k 4 rows,
Change to size 20 needles and cream yarn,
Next row: work twice into each st (28sts),
Next row: p,
Work stripes
Cont in st st, work 2 rows navy then 2 rows cream,
using navy yarn, inc 1 st at each end of the next row, then p 1 row,
cont now with cream yarn and st st, inc 1 st at each end of the foll 5th row, then each end of the [foll 6th row] twice, (36sts),
Work 3 rows without shaping
Shape top
Dec 1 st at each end of every row until there are 8sts, then cast off.
Work a second sleeve to match.

COLLAR

Using size 21 needles and navy yarn cast on 24sts and k 2 rows,
Change to size 20 needles
Next row: k,

Next row: k2, p to last 2 sts k2,
Rep the last 2 rows 4 more times,
Divide for neck
Next row: k10, cast off 4sts and k to end
Next row: k2, p6, p2tog, turn,
cont on these last sts only to complete left side
of collar
Next row: k5, turn,
Next row: sl1, p to end,
Work 4 rows without shaping,
Next row: k2tog, k3, k2tog, k2,
Work 3 rows st st
Next row: k2tog, k1, k2tog, k2,
Next row: k2, p5,
Next row: k2tog, k1, k2tog,
Next row: p3tog, fasten off.
Return to rem sts, with WS facing, rejoin yarn
Next row: p2tog, p4, turn, sl1, k to end,
Work 5 rows without shaping,
Next row: k2, k2tog, k3, k2tog,
Work 3 rows straight,
Next row: k2, k2tog, k1, k2tog,
Next row: p3, k2,
Next row: k2tog, k1, k2tog,
Next row: p3tog, fasten off.

DECORATIVE BOW

Using size 20 needles and some red sewing
thread, cast on 40sts, then using a larger needle,
cast them off again very loosely.

MATCHING BLOOMERS

LEG

Using size 21 needles and navy yarn cast on
40sts, and k 2 rows,
Change to size 20 needles, beg with a k row and
work 20 rows in st st
Inc 1 st at each end of the next 4 rows, then cast
off 2 sts at the beg of the next 4 rows, leave sts
on a spare needle.
Work a second leg to match.
Join legs
Make sure that you have the RS of both legs
facing you. Knit across the sts of the second leg
then cont across the sts from the spare needle,
(80sts)
Cont in st st for 17 more rows,
Cast off.

TO MAKE UP

Bag out, block and steam the pieces following the instructions in the
section on finishing (page 6).

Join the side seams of the dress.

Stitch enough of the shoulder seams to enable the sleeves to be put in,
but leave the rest of the shoulder seam open, this can be finished when
the dress is on the doll.

Join the underarm seams of the sleeves and stitch the sleeves into place.

Run a gathering thread of elastic round the waist (where the navy skirt
meets the cream top) and pull up to fit.

Put the dress on the doll, then carefully finish shoulder seams and stitch
the collar in place, adding the decorative bow to the centre front of
collar.

Join each leg seam of the bloomers, then the centre back and crotch
seam. Run a gathering thread of elastic round the waistline and draw
up to fit. Repeat for the hem edge of each leg.

The tight edge of each leg should fit above the knee over black
stockings.

Boy's Sailor Suit

The jacket is a bit of a cheat, the front is knitted in one piece with a button band up the centre to look as if it fastens. When the collar is attached it should look as if the jacket is being worn over a simple shirt or vest.

Materials
- A pair each of size 20 and size 21 needles
- 50m reel of Gütermann pure silk S303, in cream (col 802)
- 50m reel of Gütermann pure silk S303, in navy (col 339)
- A small red ribbon bow, or a small amount of red sewing thread for a knitted one
- Four tiny button beads

Tension
9sts and 11 rows equal 1cm (⅜in), using size 20 needles over st st

JACKET

BACK
Using size 21 needles and cream yarn, cast on 33sts and k 2 rows,
Change to size 20 needles and in st st work 36 rows,

Shape armholes
Cast off 2sts at the beg of the next 2 rows, then dec 1 st at each end of the foll 2 rows (25sts)
Work straight for 15 rows,

Shape shoulders
Next row: p21, turn,
Next row: sl1, k16, turn,
Next row: sl 1, p to end,
Cast off.

FRONT
Using size 21 needles and cream yarn, cast on 18sts and k 2 rows,
Change to size 20 needles,
Next row: k to end,
Next row: p to last 3sts, k3,
Rep these 2 rows 6 times more,
Next row: k to end,
Next row: p to last 3sts, cast off 3, break off yarn to finish last st, and leave sts on a spare needle.

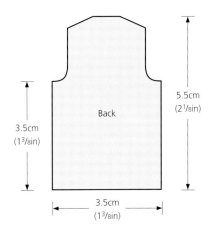

Back
5.5cm (2¹⁄₈in)
3.5cm (1³⁄₈in)
3.5cm (1³⁄₈in)

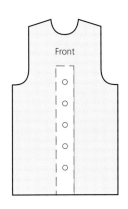

Front

Next row: k2tog, k4, turn,
Next row: sl1, p2, p2tog, turn,
Cast off rem 8sts.
Return to rem sts, with WS facing rejoin yarn,
Next row: p2tog, p5, turn,
Next row: sl1, k3, k2tog, turn,
Next row: p2tog, p to end,
Cast of rem 8sts.

SLEEVE

Using size 21 needles and navy yarn, cast on 18sts,
Change to cream yarn, beg with a k row, work 4 rows st st, change to navy yarn work 2 rows st st,
Change to size 20 needles and cream yarn,
Inc row: k4, [inc twice into next st] 10 times, k4, (28sts)
Next row: p
Cont in st st as set, but inc 1 st at each end of the 3rd row and then each foll 6th row, until there are 36sts, work 3 rows straight, finish with a WS row,
Shape top
Dec 1 st at each end of every row until 8sts rem,
Cast off.
Work a second sleeve to match.

COLLAR

Using size 21 needles and navy yarn, cast on 24sts and k 2 rows,
Change to size 20 needles,
Next row: k,
Next row: k2, p to last 2 sts k2,
Cont in patt as now set for 10 more rows
Next row: k10, cast off 4, k to end,
Next row: k2, p6, p2tog, turn,
Cont on these sts only to complete LS of neck,

Using size 21 needles and cream yarn, cast on 18sts and k 2 rows,
Change to size 20 needles,
Next row: k to end,
Next row: k3, p to end.
Rep these 2 rows 7 more times,
Join fronts
Knit across the next row, then with RS facing k across the sts from spare needle (33sts)
Next row: p15, k3, p15,
Next row: k to end
Next row: p15, k3, p15,
Rep the last 2 rows 8 times more
Shape armholes
Keeping patt correct cast off 2sts at the beg of the next 2 rows, then dec 1 st at each end of the next 2 rows (25sts)
Patt 2 rows,
Work now in plain st st (without the centre button band) for 12 rows,
Shape neck and shoulders
Next row: k11, cast off 3, k to end,
Next row: p9, p2tog, turn,

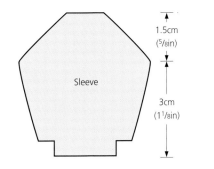

Sleeve
1.5cm (⁵⁄₈in)
3cm (1¹⁄₈in)

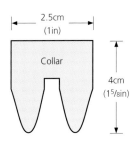

Collar
2.5cm (1in)
4cm (1⁵⁄₈in)

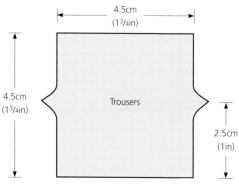

4.5cm
(1³/₄in)

4.5cm
(1³/₄in)

Trousers

2.5cm
(1in)

Next row: k5, turn, sl1, p to end,
Next row: k,
Cont in patt without shaping for 3 rows,
Shape point
Next row: k2tog, k3, k2tog, k2,
Next row: k2, p to end,
Next row: k,
Next row: k2, p to end,
Next row: k2tog, k3, k2tog,
Next row: p,
Next row: k2tog, k1, k2tog,
Next row: p3tog, fasten off.
With WS facing return to rem sts, rejoin yarn
Next row: p2tog, p4, turn, sl1, k4,
Next row: p to last 3sts, k3,
Work 4 rows straight,
Next row: k2, k2tog, k3, k2tog,
Next row: p to last 3sts, k3,
Work 2 rows straight,
Next row: k2tog, k3, k2tog,
Next row: p,
Next row: k2tog, k1, k2tog,
Next row: p3tog, fasten off.

BELT

Using size 21 needles, cast on 5sts,
Next row: k1, p1, k1, p1, k1,
Rep this row until belt measures 6cm (2³/₈in),
cast off.

BOW

Using size 20 needles and any available red thread, cast on 40sts, then very loosely cast them off again.

TROUSERS

Follow the instructions for the Girl's Sailor Suit Bloomers but, when making up, let them hang straight: do not gather up the bottom of the legs.

TO MAKE UP

Bag out, block and steam the pieces following the instructions in the section on finishing (page 6).

On the front, fold the bottom bit of the button band left over right, and catch down the cast off edge.

Join the side seams of the jacket, and enough of the shoulder seams to enable the sleeves to be attached. Join the underarm seam of each sleeve and stitch sleeves in place.

Put the jacket on the doll and complete the shoulder seams. Place the points of the collar at the top edge of the button band, and carefully stitch into place on the front of the jacket and round the back neck. The front collar should form a 'V' shape, with a white 'vest' showing at the neck.

Place the belt round the doll just below waist level and stitch together at the centre back. Stitch on small buckle or bead buttons. Stitch bead buttons on the centre-front button band. Attach bow to the front collar.

Stitch leg seams of trousers, then centre-front and back seams. Place a gathering thread of fine elastic round the waist, and draw up to fit.

I Do Like to Be Beside the Seaside

*The famous music hall song was written by
John A. Glover-Kind in 1907*

Oh! I do like to be beside the seaside

I do like to be beside the sea!

I do like to stroll upon the prom, prom, prom

Where the brass bands play

Tiddely-om-pom-pom!

So just let me be beside the seaside –

I'll be beside myself with glee.

And there's lots of girls beside

I should like to be beside

Beside the seaside,

Beside the sea!

Party time

Like the afternoon version, the gown worn in the evenings reflected the exuberant spirit of the age as set by the court of Edward and Alexandria. Evening dresses were picturesque, romantic, elaborate, frothy, fairy-like creations, giving the impression of being designed for a summer garden party. They were made from sumptuous silk, crêpe de Chine, chiffon and tulle fabrics with a plethora of applied

'It is impossible to go to any party without noting the costumes worn by women, in many cases quite out of proportion in cost with the incomes enjoyed'
Berrow's Worcester Journal, August 1901

decoration in the form of bows, flowers, ruched ribbon, frills, fringing and lace. Edwardian ladies had a passion for lace, which was used in abundance on both day and evening wear. The colours for evening echoed the soft, pastel, chalky, flower colours of the tea-gown.

The evening-dress and the tea-gown may well have had many similarities, but in design and styling there was one major difference: evening-dresses were extravagantly décolleté. The high boned collar was abandoned.

The most popular necklines were very low and either off the shoulder

Crowds watching a balloon race in July, 1906. Although women were covered from chin to ankle even on festive occasions such as this, for formal evening parties the dress code demanded bare arms and very low necklines.

or supported with narrow shoulder straps. Sleeves were non-existent or very short. Bare necks, shoulders and arms were the accepted norm for formal evenings. Ankles, of course, were still hidden underneath a floor-length, swishing skirt, and its long, full train.

To complete an outfit an elaborate hair ornament would adorn the piled-high hair, a corsage or jewelled ornament would be worn at the waist, and hands would be covered by long white gloves. A fan, often made of ostrich feathers, was an essential accessory.

Evening wear for those elite members of high society who were entitled to attend court functions was subjected to a very strict correct dress code, and full evening dress was always worn. For ladies this consisted of a long dress (which for young debutantes had to be white), with a long separate train attached either to the shoulders or the waist. An exotic head-dress had to be worn, made of three white ostrich feathers and a tulle veil. Long white gloves, a fan and a bouquet of flowers were further compulsory accessories.

The correct formal dress for gentlemen was the morning suit, which was worn for evening, dinner parties and weddings. The suit consisted of a single-breasted jacket with three or four buttons and high lapels. The skirt of the jacket was cut away at the front to slope to the back, forming two knee-length tails. The jacket was worn open or fastened by a single button. The trousers were long and narrow.

The suit was worn with a white shirt that had a starched high, wing or butterfly collar, and a white single-breasted waistcoat. For evenings a white bow tie was worn.

LADY'S EVENING GOWN

Materials
- A pair each of size 20 and size 21 needles
- Two 100m reels of Gütermann pure silk S303, in pale green (col 924)
- Narrow silk ribbon for decoration

Tension
9sts and 11 rows equal 1cm (⅜in), using size 20 needles over st st

Abbreviations
m1: (make one stitch), pick up the thread that is stretched between the needles, and knit into the back loop of it

LACE PATTERN
1st row: k3, yrn, p2tog, k4, yrn, p2tog, k2,
2nd row: k4, yrn, p2tog, k1, p2tog, yo, k4,
3rd row: k5, yrn, p2tog, k2, yrn, p2tog, k2,
4th row: k4, yrn, p2tog, k2, yrn, p2tog, k3,
5th row: cast off 3sts, yfwd, k5, yrn, p2tog, k2,
6th row: k4, yrn, p2tog, k4, yfwd, (k1, p1) into last st

SKIRT
Using size 20 needles, cast on 88sts, and p 1 row,
1st row: 1st row of lace patt, k to end,
2nd row: k2, p73, 2nd row of lace patt,
3rd row: 3rd row of lace patt, k to end,
4th row: k2, p73, 4th row of lace patt,
5th row: 5th row of lace patt, k2tog, k to end,
6th row: k2, p72, 6th row of lace patt,
Work 3 more repeats of the patt as established, but on every 5th patt row ktog, the 2 sts, immediately following the lace patt,
Work 1 more repeat of the patt but now work the dec on each RS row instead of the 5th patt row, (81sts)
Shape hip darts
Next row: 1st row of lace patt, k60 turn,
Next row: sl1, p59, 2nd row of lace patt,
Next row: 3rd row of lace patt, k52, turn,
Next row: sl1, p51, 4th row of lace patt,
Next row: 5th row of lace patt, k to end,
Next row: k2, p66, 6th row of lace patt,
Rep the last 6 rows twice more,
Now keeping the lace hem correct, work 10 rows without shaping,
11th row: 5th row of lace patt, [yfwd, k2tog] 9 times, p to end,
12th row: k2, p66, 6th row of lace patt,
Shape hem godet
Keeping lace patt correct at all times,
1st row: lace patt, turn,
2nd and all alt rows: sl1, patt to end,
3rd row: lace patt, k14, turn,
5th row: lace patt, k12, turn,
7th row: lace patt, turn,
9th row: lace patt, k10, turn,
11th row: lace patt, k8, turn,
13th row: lace patt, turn,
15th row: lace patt, k6, turn,
17th row: lace patt, k4, turn,
19th row: lace patt, turn,
21st row: lace patt, k2, turn,
23rd row: lace patt, [yfwd, k2tog] to last 2sts, k2,
24th row: k2, patt to end,
rep rows 1 to 22 once more,
Next row: lace patt, [yfwd, k2tog] 9 times, p to end,
Next row: k2, patt to end,
Keeping lace patt correct work 12 rows without shaping,
Shape hip darts
1st row: lace patt, k52, turn,
2nd row: sl1, patt to end,
3rd row: lace patt, k60, turn,
4th row: sl1, patt to end,
5th row: lace patt, k to end,
6th row: k2, patt to end,
Rep the last 6 rows, twice more,
Shape back hem
Next row: lace patt, m1, k to end,
Keeping lace patt correct, m1 stitch in this way on each of the next 3 RS rows, then on each [lace patt 1st row], of the next 4 patt reps, (88sts)
Work back godet
1st row: 1st row of lace patt, [yfwd, k2tog] 16 times, k to end,
2nd row: k2, patt to end,
3rd row: 3rd row of lace patt, k30, turn,
4th row and foll alt rows: sl1, patt to end,
5th row: 5th row of lace patt, k26, turn,
7th row: 1st row of lace patt, turn,
9th row: 3rd row of lace patt, k22, turn,

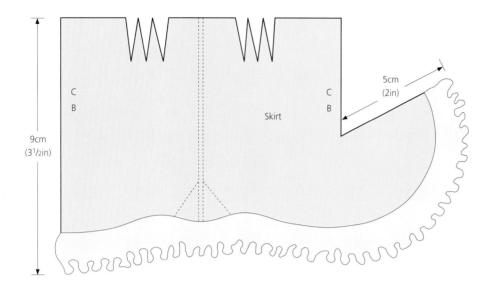

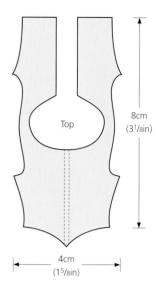

11th row: 5th row of lace patt, k18, turn,
13th row: 1st row of lace patt, turn,
15th row: 3rd row of lace patt, k14, turn,
17th row: 5th row of lace patt, k10, turn,
19th row: 1st row of lace patt, turn,
21st row: 3rd row of lace patt, k6, turn,
23rd row: 5th row of lace patt, k2, turn,
25th row: 1st row of lace patt, turn,
27th row: 3rd row of lace patt, [yfwd, k2tog] 16 times, turn,
29th row: 5th row of lace patt, k30, turn,
30th row: sl1, patt to end,
Cont in this way, turning after the lace patt on each 1st row of lace patt, and working 4sts, less on each RS row, until the 2 rows, (k2, turn; sl1, patt to end), have been worked
Next row: 5th row of lace patt, [yfwd, k2tog] 17 times, turn,
Next row: sl1, patt to end,
Next row: 1st row of lace patt, turn,
Next row: sl1, patt to end,
Next row: 3rd row of lace patt, k30, turn,
Next row: sl1, patt to end,
Work as ** to **
Next row: 1st row of lace patt, turn,
Next row: sl1, patt to end,
Next row: 3rd row of lace patt, [yfwd, k2tog] 16 times,
Next row: sl1, patt to end,
Next row: 5th row of lace patt, k30, turn,
Next row: sl1, patt to end,
Work as ** to ** once more,

Next row: 5th row of lace patt, [yfwd, k2tog] 16 times, k to end,
Next row: k2, patt to end,
Cast off.

BODICE

FRONT

Using size 20 needles, cast on 33sts, and k 1 row,
Next row: k4, inc into next st, k8, k2tog, yfwd, sl2tog-k1-p2sso, yfwd, ssk, k7, inc into next st, k5,
Next row: k to end,
Rep last 2 rows, once more,
Next row: k4, inc into next st, k8, k2tog, yfwd, sl2tog-k1-p2sso, yfwd, ssk, k7, inc into next st, k5,
Next row: p to end,
Rep the last 2 rows, twice more,
Next row: inc into first st, k3, inc into next st, k8, k2tog, yfwd, sl2tog-k1-p2sso, yfwd, ssk, k7, inc into next st, k4, inc into last st,
Next row: p
Next row: k16, yfwd, sl2tog-k1-p2sso, yfwd, k to end,
Next row: p
The last 2 rows form the patt, cont in patt, but at the same time inc 1 st at each end of the next row, and each end of the foll 4th row, then work 3 rows straight,
Shape armholes
Cast off 2sts at the beg of the next 2 rows, dec 1 st at each end of the foll row, then patt straight

for 7 rows,

Shape neck

Next row: k12, cast off 9sts, k to end,

Next row: p12, turn,

Cont on these last 12sts, to work R neck and shoulder,

1st row: ssk, k to last st, inc into last st,

Next 3 rows: dec 1st at the neck edge of each row,

Rep last 4 rows once more,

Next row: ssk, k to last st inc into last st,

Work straight for 5 rows

Shape back neck

1st row: inc into first st, k to last 2sts, k2tog,

Next 3 rows: inc 1 st at the neck edge of each row,

Rep the last 4 rows, once more,

Next row: cast on 2sts, k to last 2sts, k2tog,

Work without shaping for 7 rows,

Shape armhole

Inc 1 st at the end of the next row, cast on 2sts at the beg of the foll row.

Cont in st st, and shape sides by dec 1 st at the end of the 5th row, then the end of the [foll 4th row] twice, work 7 rows straight, then k 2 rows and cast off.

With the WS facing return to the rem sts, rejoin yarn and p to end,

Shape left side of neck

Next row: inc into 1st st, k to last 2 sts, k2tog,

Next 3 rows: dec 1 st at the neck edge of each row,

Next row: inc into 1st, k to last 2sts, k2tog

Rep the last 4 rows once more, then work 5 rows straight,

1st row: k2tog, k to last st, inc into last st,

Next 3 rows: inc 1 st at the neck edge of each row,

Repeat the last 4 rows, once more,

Next row: k2tog, k to end,

Cast on 2sts at the beg of the next row and p to end, then work 6 rows straight,

Shape armhole

Inc 1 st at beg of next row, then cast on 2sts at beg of foll alt row.

Cont in st st but at the same time, dec 1 st at the beg of the [foll 4th row] 3 times, work 7 rows, straight, then k 2 rows and cast off.

SLEEVES

Using size 21 needles, cast on 7sts and k 1 row,

1st row: k3, yrn, p2tog, k2,

2nd row: k1, p2tog, yfwd, k4,

3rd row: k5, yrn, p2tog,

4th row: k2, yrn, p2tog, k3,

5th row: cast off 3sts, yfwd, k3,

6th row: k4, yfwd, [k1, p1] into last st

These 6 rows form the patt, work a total of 6 reps of the patt for each sleeve.

DECORATIVE ROSES

Large (make one for each shoulder)

Using size 21 needles, cast on 25sts,

1st row: k2, sl1, [k4, sl1] 4 times, k2,

2nd row: p2, sl1, [p4, sl1] 4 times, p2.

Repeat the 2 rows twice more.

Break off the yarn. Thread the end of yarn through the sts, pull up tightly and secure.

Small (for the neck you will need 6 for the front and 5 for the back)

Using size 21 needles cast on 12 sts,

1st row: k1, sl1, [k2, sl1] 3 times, k1,

2nd row: p1, sl1, [p2, sl1] 3 times, p1,

Rep the 2 rows once more.

Break off yarn. Thread the end of the yarn through the sts, pull up tightly and secure.

TO MAKE UP

Bag out, block and steam the pieces following the instructions in the section on finishing (page 6).

Skirt. Join the centre-back seam.

Run a length of either contrast or matching silk ribbon through the eyelet holes down the centre front. Put the skirt on the doll, gather the waist to fit.

Bodice. Join the side seams, thread a silk ribbon through the eyelet holes.

Decorate the neckline by stitching a length of ruched ribbon round the edge, and add some knitted or silk roses.

When the bodice is on the doll, stitch up the centre-back seam.

Add decorations to the centre-front and back godets.

MORNING SUIT

The tails of the jacket are knitted separately then joined together at the waist. The bodice part is knitted in one piece until the armholes are reached. At this point the left front, the back and then the right front are completed.

Materials
- A pair each of size 19 and size 20 needles
- Four 30m reels of Gütermann polyester top-stitching thread in black (col 000)
- Six beads or tiny buttons
- a very small amount of white silk or cotton sewing thread for pocket hankie

Tension
8sts and 9.25 rows equal 1cm (⅜in), using size 19 needles over st st

JACKET

POCKET
Using size 20 needles, cast on 5sts, beg with a k row and work 5 rows in st st, leave sts on a spare needle

LEFT TAIL
Using size 20 needles cast on 12sts and k 1 row, Change to size 19 needles
Next row: k to last 2sts, m1, k2,
Next row: k2, m1, p to last 4 sts, k4,
Rep the last 2 rows, 3 times more
cont to inc inside the 2 edge sts, as set, on each foll 3rd row until there are 35sts, work 1 row to finish with a WS row,
Next row: k23, k2tog, k to end,
Next row: k2, m1, p to last 4sts, k4,
Next row: k to end
Next row: k2, p to last 4sts, k4,
Next row: k22, k2tog, k10, m1, k2,
Next row: k2, p6, turn,
Next row: sl1, k7,
Next row: k2, p2, turn,
Next row: sl1, p3,
Next row: cast on 9sts, k the 9sts plus the next 2sts, p to last 4sts, cast off 4, and fasten off. Leave sts on a spare needle.

RIGHT TAIL

Using size 20 needles cast on 12sts, and k 1 row.
Change to size 19 needles
Next row: k2, m1, k to end,
Next row: k4, p to last 2sts, m1, k2,
Rep the last 2 rows, 3 times more
cont to inc inside the 2 edge sts, as set, on each
foll 3rd row until there are 35sts, work 1 row to
finish with a WS row,
Next row: k10, k2tog, k to end,
Next row: k4, p to last 2 sts, m1, k2,
Next row: k to end,
Next row: k4, p to last 2sts, k2,
Next row: k2, m1, k5, turn,
Next row: sl1, p5, k2,
Next row: k4, turn,
Next row: sl1, p1, k2,
Next row: k12, k2tog, k to end,
Next row: k4, p to last 2sts, k2,

Join the tails
Cast on 9 sts, p the 9sts, then k across the rest
of the right tail sts, with the RS facing cont to k
across the sts from spare needle. (84sts)
Next row: k2, p to last 2sts, k2,

Shape waist and lapels
1st row: k2, m1, k to last 2 sts, m1, k2,
2nd and all alt rows: k2, p to last 2sts, k2,
3rd row: K2, m1, k20, m1, k42, m1, k20, m1, k2,
5th row: k2, m1, k to last 2 sts, m1, k2,
7th row: k to end,
9th row: k2, m1, k22, k2tog, k44, k2tog, k22,
m1, k2,
11th row: k2, m1, k to last 2 sts, m1, k2,
12th row: k2, p to last 2sts, k2,

Divide for armholes
Next row: k2, m1, k22, cast off 4, k the next 37
sts, cast off 4, k the next 21sts, m1, k2,

Work left front
Next row: k3, p22, turn
Next row: cast off 2, k to last 3sts, p1, k2,
Next row: k3, p to last st, p2tog,
Next row: k2tog, k last 4sts, p2, k2,
Next row: k4, p to end,
Next row: k17, p2, k2,
Next row: k4, p to end,
Next row: k16, p3, k2,
Next row: k5, p to end

Add pocket
Next row: k4, cast off 5, k the next 6, p3, k2
Next row: k5, p7, with the WS facing, p across
the sts from the pocket backing, to replace the
cast off sts, then p to end,
Cont straight keeping patt correct, but working

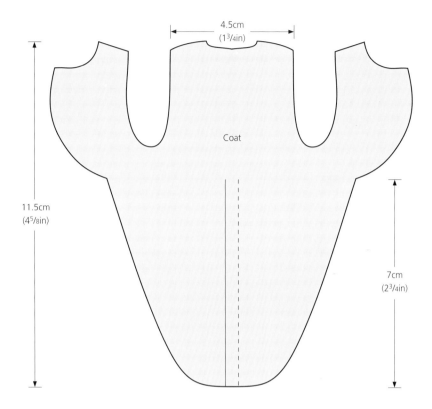

4.5cm
(1³/₄in)

11.5cm
(4⁵/₈in)

Coat

7cm
(2³/₄in)

an extra purl st inside the garter edge of the next
row, then [the foll 4th row] twice,

Shape neck
Next row: cast off 8, p to end,
Next row: k to end,
Next row: cast off 2, k the next 5, turn,
Next row: sl1, k3, k2tog,
Next row: p to end,
Cast off.
Return to rem sts, with WS facing rejoin yarn,
cast off 2sts, p the next 35sts, turn, cont on
these 36sts only.
Next row: cast off 2, k to end,
Next row: p2tog, p to last 2sts, p2tog,
cont in st st without shaping for 18 rows,

Shape shoulders
Next row: k26, turn,
Next row: sl1, k5, cast off 10, k the next 5, turn,
Next row: sl1, k3, k2tog, turn,
Next row: sl1, k9,
Cast off,
Return to sts for left shoulder. With RS facing
rejoin yarn,
Next row: k2tog, k to end,
Next row: p to end,
Cast off.

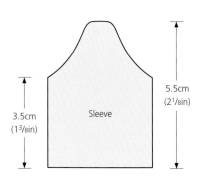

3.5cm
(1³/₈in)

Sleeve

5.5cm
(2¹/₈in)

Work right front
Return to the rem sts, with WS facing rejoin yarn,
Next row: cast off 2, p next 19, k3,
Next row: k2, p1, k to last 2sts, k2tog,
Next row: p2tog, p to last 3 sts, k3,
cont without shaping, keeping the patt correct,
but working an extra purl st inside the garter
edge as set, on the next row, then [every foll 4th
row] 4 times,
Shape neck and shoulder
Next row: cast off 8, k the next 7, turn,
Next row: sl1, k7,
Next row: cast off 2sts, k the next 10,
Next row: p to last 2sts, p2tog,
Cast off.

SLEEVE
Using size 20 needles cast on 32sts and k 1 row,
Change to size 19 needles, beg with a k row,
work 32 rows in st st,
Shape top
Cast off 2sts at the beg of the next 4 rows,
Dec 1 st at each end of the next 6 RS rows, then
each end of the foll p row,
Cast off rem 10 sts.
Work a second sleeve to match.

TO MAKE UP

Bag out, block and steam the pieces following the instructions in the section on finishing (page 6).

Slip st the 3 sides of the pocket backing in place.

Join shoulder seams.

Place the RS of the collar to the WS of the jacket, matching the centre of the collar cast-off edge to the centre of the back neck. Begin and end by stitching 2 or 3 stitches of the short edge of the collar to the lapel cast-off sts to form a 'V' shape when the lapel is folded back.

At the centre-back waist, fold the garter stitch edge of the right tail over the left tail and slip stitch the cast-off edge on the underside.

Join the underarm seam of each sleeve, and stitch the sleeves into place.

Add 2 beads or buttons to each front, 2 to the outside edge of each sleeve and 2 to the top of the vent at centre back.

Knit a small square in white silk or sewing cotton, and pop it into the breast pocket.

COLLAR
Using size 20 needles, cast on 28sts, and k 1 row,
Change to size 19 needles
Next row: k to end,
Next row: k3, p to last 3sts, k3,
Rep last 2 rows once more,
Next row: k3, k2tog, k18, k2tog, k3,
Next row: k3, p to last 3sts, k3,
Next row: k to last 4sts, turn, sl1, p to last 4sts,
turn,
Next row: sl1, k12, turn, sl1, p to end,
Next row: k3, k2tog, k16, k2tog, k3,
Cast off.

SINGLE-BREASTED EVENING WAISTCOAT

The front of the waistcoat is knitted in moss st, which is a reversible fabric, so there are only instructions for one front. For the other front, knit an identical piece and just turn it over.

Materials
● A pair each of size 20 and size 21 needles
● 50m reel of Gütermann pure silk, S303, in white, (col 800)
● Four tiny beads or buttons

Tension
8sts and 14 rows equal 1cm (⅜in), using size 20 needles over moss st

FRONT
Using size 20 needles, cast on 1 st,
Next row: k1, p1, k1 into the st,
Next row: cast on 2sts, k1, [p1, k1] to end,
Next row: cast on 2sts, k1, [p1, k1] to end,
Rep last 2 rows once more,
Next row: cast on 3sts, [p1, k1] to end
Next row: cast on 2sts, [k1, p1], to end,
Next row: cast on 5sts, k1, [p1, k1] to end,

(21sts)
Next row: k1, [p1, k1] to end, Cont in moss st without shaping for a further 29 rows,
Shape neck
Keeping patt correct dec 1 st at the beg of the next row, and the same edge of the foll 6th row, finish at armhole edge
Shape armhole
Cast off 2 sts at beg of the next row and the foll alt row,
Keeping patt correct dec 1 st at the beg (neck edge) of the foll 3rd row, then each foll 6th row until there are 10sts, work one row to finish at neck edge,
Next row: patt 5, turn, sl1, patt to end,
Cast off.
Work a second front to match.

BACK
Using size 20 needles cast on 36sts and k 2 rows,
Beg with a k row, work 26 rows st st,
Shape armholes
Cast off 2 sts at the beg of the next 4 rows,
Cont in st st without shaping for 20 rows,
Shape shoulders and neck
Next row: k23, turn,
Next row: sl1, p3, cast off 10, p the next 3, turn,
Next row: sl1, k3, turn,
Cast off rem 9sts,
Return to rem sts, with RS facing rejoin yarn and k to end, then cast off.

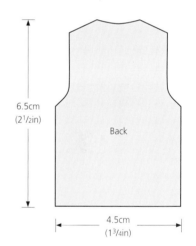

6.5cm
(2½in)

Back

4.5cm
(1¾in)

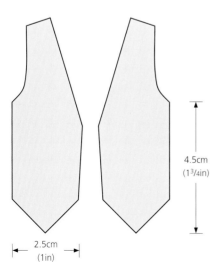

4.5cm
(1¾in)

2.5cm
(1in)

TO MAKE UP

Bag out, block and steam the pieces following the instructions in the section on finishing (page 6).

Join the shoulder and side seams.

Fold the fronts left over right, just enough for a button band. Attach beads or tiny buttons.

BOY'S PARTY SUIT

This suit is a version of the Norfolk suit, but it is knitted in mercerised cotton to give a slight shine reminiscent of velvet. The lace collar and cuffs help to convert it into party mood.

Materials

- A pair each of size 19 and size 20 needles
- 10g ball of DMC Cotton perlé, 12, in black (col 310)
- 50m reel of Gütermann pure silk S303, in white, (col 800)

Tension

7sts and 9.5 rows equal 1cm (⅜in) using size 19 needles over st st

JACKET

BACK

Using size 20 needles and cotton, cast on 25sts, and k 3 rows.

Change to size 19 needles, beg with a k row and work 2 rows in st st. Cont. in st st as set, and dec 1 st at each end of the next row and the foll 4th row, work 1 row straight, then inc 1 st at each end of the next row and the foll 4th row, (25sts).

Cont without shaping for 3 more rows,

Shape armholes

Dec 1 st at each end of the next 3 rows, then work straight for 13 rows,

Shape shoulders

Next row: k16sts, turn,
Next row: sl1, p3, cast off 5, p the next 3sts, turn,
Next row: sl1, k1, k2tog, turn,
Next row: cast off 6sts.

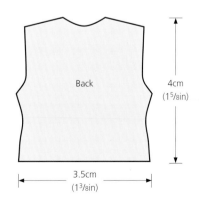

Back

4cm
(1⁵⁄₈in)

3.5cm
(1³⁄₈in)

Return to rem sts with WS facing rejoin yarn, k2tog, k to end then cast off.

RIGHT FRONT

Using size 20 needles and cotton cast on18sts and k 3 rows,
Change to size 19 needles,
1st row: k8, p2, k to end,
2nd row: p8, k2, p5, k3,
These 2 rows form the patt and are used throughout. Keeping patt as set
dec 1 st at end of the next row and the foll 4th row.
Work 1 row straight, then inc 1 st at the end of the next row and the foll 4th row.
Work 3 rows straight,
Shape armholes
Dec 1 st at the end of the next row and the same edge of the foll 2 rows.
Work straight for 11 more rows to finish at neck edge,
Shape neck
Cast off 4sts at the beg of next row, and dec 1 st at the end of the foll row,
Next row: k2tog, k2, p2, turn,
Next row: sl1, k1, p1, p2tog, turn,
Cast off 8sts.

LEFT FRONT

Using size 20 needles and cotton, cast on18sts and k 3 rows,
Change to size 19 needles,
1st row: k8, p2, k to end,
2nd row: k3, p5, k2, p to end,
These 2 rows form the patt and are used throughout, keeping patt as set dec 1 st at the beg of the next row and the foll 4th row,
Work 1 row straight, then inc 1 st at the beg of the next row and the foll 4th row,
Work 3 rows straight,

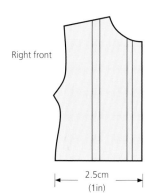

Right front

2.5cm
(1in)

Shape armholes
Dec 1 st at the beg of the next row and the same edge of the foll 2 rows,
Work straight for 10 more rows to finish at neck edge,
Shape neck
Cast off 4sts at the beg of next row, and dec 1 st at the end of the foll row,
Next row: p2tog, p1, k2, p1, turn,
Next row: sl1, p2, k2tog, turn,
Cast off 8sts.

SLEEVES

Using size 20 needles and cotton, cast on 18sts, and k 3 rows,
Change to size 19 needles, beg with a k row and work in st st as folls,
inc 1 st at each end of the next row, then each end of foll 4th row, then [the foll 6th row] twice, finish with a WS row, (26sts)
Shape top
Dec 1 st at each end of every row until 6 sts rem, cast off.
Work a second sleeve to match.

BELT

Using size 20 needles and cotton cast on 3 sts,
Next row: k1, p1, k1,
Rep this row until belt measures 6cm (2⅜in),
Next row: k3tog, fasten off.

COLLAR

Using size 20 needles and white silk, cast on 6sts and k 2 rows,
1st row: k1, yfwd, ssk, k1, yfwd, yrn, k1, yfwd, k1,
2nd row: k4, p1, k2, turn,
3rd row: k to end,
4th row: cast off 3sts, k the next 3, p1,
Rep these 4 rows, 13 times more, k2 rows, cast off.

LACE CUFFS

Using size 20 needles and white silk yarn, cast on 3sts and k1 row,
1st row: k1, [yfwd, yrn, k1] twice,
2nd row: [k2, p1] twice, k1,
3rd row: sl1, yfwd, sl1-k1-psso, k4,
4th row: cast off 4sts, p1, k1, Repeat these 4 rows, 5 times more, k1 row, cast off.
Work a second piece to match.

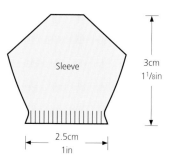

Sleeve

3cm
1⅛in

2.5cm
1in

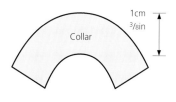

Collar

1cm
⅜in

TROUSERS

LEG

Using size 20 needles and cotton cast on 30 sts, and k4 rows,
Change to size 19 needles,
Beg with a k row, work in st st for 20 rows,
Cast off 2 sts at the beg of the next 4 rows, then cont straight for 10 more rows. Cast off.
Work a second leg to match.

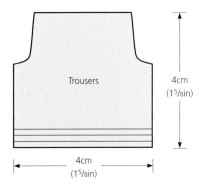

Trousers

4cm (1⁵/₈in)

4cm (1⁵/₈in)

TO MAKE UP

Bag out, block and steam the pieces following the instructions on finishing (page 6).

Join each sleeve underarm seam. Stitch each lace cuff into a circle, then slip stitch the cuff just inside the wrist end of the sleeve.

Stitch jacket shoulder and side seams. Stitch each sleeve into place, matching the shoulder seams to the centre of sleeve cast-off edge.

Beg and end 2sts in from the centre-front edge of the neck, and carefully over-sew the collar inner edge to the jacket neckline.

Put jacket on doll, fold fronts left over right and sew on small beads for buttons. Place belt around waist, again folding left over right. Sew on buckle or small beads as fasteners. Decorate outside edge of sleeve with 2 beads.

Stitch the inside trouser leg seams, then join the crotch from front to back. Run a gathering thread round the waist and draw up to fit.

GIRL'S PARTY DRESS

This sweet pea coloured party dress has a lace trimmed bodice and a two tiered lace skirt. The belt and collar are knitted in a toning colour, and the under-skirt has been knitted to match.

Materials
- A pair each of size 20 and size 21 needles
- 100m reel of Gütermann pure silk, S303, in mauve (col 158)
- A small amount of Gütermann pure silk, S303, in pink (col 659)
- Narrow silk ribbon for bow decoration

Tension
9sts and 11 rows equal 1cm (⅜in), using size 20 needles over st st

SKIRT

LONG LACE-TIER
Using size 20 needles and mauve silk cast on 42sts and k 1 row
Preparation row: k2, p21, yo, k2tog, k3, [yrn, p2tog] twice, yrn, p3tog, yrn, p5, 2yrn, p2tog,
1st row: yrn, k2, p1, k3, k2tog, yfwd, k12, yfwd, k2tog, K21,
2nd row: k2, p21, yo, k2tog, k3, [yrn, p2tog] 3 times, p2, yrn, p2tog, p2, [2yrn, p2tog] twice,
3rd row: [k2, p1] twice, k1, k2tog, yfwd, k14, yfwd, k2tog, k19, turn,
4th row: sl1, p20, yo, k2tog, k3, [yrn, p2tog] 3 times, [p4, yrn, p2tog] twice,
5th row: cast off 4, k the next 3sts, yfwd, k2tog, k13, yfwd, k2tog, k21,
6th row: k2, p21, yfwd, k2tog, k3, [yrn, p2tog] 3 times, p1, p2tog, yrn, p5,
7th row: k6, yfwd, k2tog, k2, yfwd, k2tog, k7, yfwd, k2tog, k19, turn,
8th row: sl1, p20, yo, k2tog, k3, [yrn, p2tog] twice, yrn, p3tog, yrn, p5, 2yrn, p2tog, (43sts)
Repeat the last 8 rows 17 times more but on the last row of the last rep, end yrn, p2tog, instead of 2yrn, p2tog, then cast off.

SHORT LACE-TIER
Using size 20 needles and mauve silk, cast on 17sts and k 1 row,

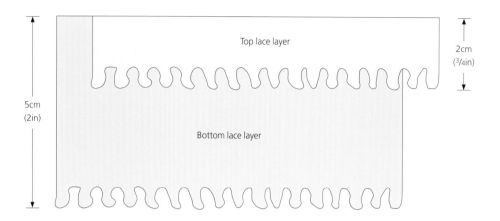

Preparation row: k3, [yrn, p2tog] twice, yrn, p3tog, yrn, p5, 2yrn, p2tog,
1st row: yrn, k2, p1, k3, k2tog, yfwd, k10
2nd row: k3, [yrn, p2tog] 3 times, p2, yrn, p2tog, p2, [2yrn, p2tog] twice,
3rd row: [k2, p1] twice, k1, k2tog, yfwd, k10, turn,
4th row: sl1, [yrn, p2tog] 3 times, [p4, yrn, p2tog] twice,
5th row: cast off 4, k next 3sts, yfwd, k2tog, k11,
6th row: k3, [yrn, p2tog] 3 times, p1, p2tog, yrn, p5,
7th row: k6, yfwd, k2tog, k2, yfwd, k2tog, k3, turn,
8th row: sl1, [yrn, p2tog] twice, yrn, p3tog, yrn, p5, 2yrn, p2tog, (18sts)
Repeat the last 8 rows 17 times more, but on the last row of the last rep, end yrn, p2tog, instead of 2yrn, p2tog, then cast off.

BODICE

Using size 20 needles and mauve silk cast on 60sts, p 1 row, then beg with a k row, work 10 rows in st st,
Divide for armholes
Next row: k14, cast off 2, k the next 27sts, cast off 2, k to end,

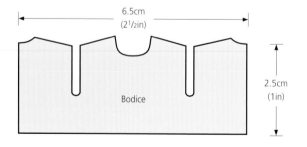

Next row: p12, p2tog, turn, cont on these 13sts only and work 13 rows in st st,
Shape shoulders and neck
Next row: p9, turn, sl1, k to end,
Next row: cast off 4, p to end,
Cast off.
Work front bodice
With WS facing return to rem sts, rejoin yarn,
Next row: p2tog, p24, p2tog, turn,
Cont on these 26sts only,
Beg with a k row, work 6 rows st st, then k3 rows, and p1 row,
Shape neck and right shoulder
Next row: k12, cast off 2, k to end,
Next row: p10, p2tog, turn,
Next row: k2tog, k to end,
Next row: p8, p2tog, turn,
Next row: k5, turn,
Next row: sl1, p4,
Cast off.
Complete left front neck and shoulder
With WS facing return to rem front bodice sts, rejoin yarn,
Next row: p2tog, p to end,
Next row: k9, k2tog,
Next row: p2tog, p4, turn,
Next row: sl1, k4, turn,
Next row: p to end,
Cast off.
Complete left back
With WS facing return to rem sts, and rejoin yarn,
Next row: p2tog, p to end,
Work 14 rows in st st,
Next row: cast off 4, k the next 4, turn,
Next row: sl1, p4,
Cast off.

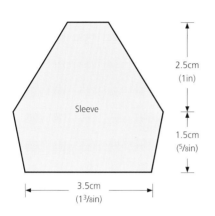

Sleeve

2.5cm
(1in)

1.5cm
(⁵/₈in)

3.5cm
(1³/₈in)

BODICE LACE TRIM

Using size 20 needles and mauve silk cast on 10 sts, and k 1 row,
Preparation row: k1, p2tog, yrn, p5, 2yrn, p2tog,
1st row: yrn, k2, p1, k3, k2tog, yfwd, k3,
2nd row: k2, p2, yrn, p2tog, p2, [2yrn, p2tog] twice,
3rd row: [k2, p1] twice, k1, k2tog, yfwd, k5,
4th row: k1, p5, yrn, p2tog, p4, yrn, p2tog,
5th row: cast off 4, k the next 3, yfwd, k2tog, k4,
6th row: k1, p2, p2tog, yrn, p5,
7th row: k6, yfwd, k2tog, k2,
8th row: k1, p2tog, yrn, p5, 2yrn, p2tog, (11sts)
Repeat the last 8 rows 3 more times, k1 row, then cast off.

COLLAR

Using size 21 needles and pink silk cast on 4sts, and p 1 row,
1st row: k2, 2yrn, p2tog,
2nd row: yrn, k2, p1, k2,
3rd row: k1, p1, [2yrn, p2tog] twice,
4th row: [k2, p1] twice, k2,
5th row: k1, p5, yrn, p2tog,
6th row: cast off 4sts, k the next 3,
Repeat these 6 rows, 7 more times, p1 row, then cast off.

SLEEVES

Using size 20 needles and mauve silk cast on 32sts, and p 1 row,
Beg with a k row, work in st st, but at the same time inc 1 st at each end of the 7th row, then the foll 6th row, work 3 rows straight,

Shape top
Dec 1 st at each end of every row until 8sts rem,
Cast off.
Work a second sleeve to match,

LACE CUFFS

Using size 20 needles and mauve silk, foll the instructions for the bodice lace trim, but work 2 lengths each of 4 repeats.

BELT

Using size 21 needles, and pink silk, cast on 6sts, and work in g st, until the band fits fairly tightly round the doll's waist,
Cast off.

TO MAKE UP

Bag out, block and steam the pieces, following the instructions in the section on finishing (page 6).

Join the underarm seams of bodice.

With the RS facing, place the short tier of the skirt on top of the long tier, matching the long straight edges. Tack the pieces together along the waist line edge, then run a gathering thread of tiny sts through both layers, and draw up to fit the waistline of the bodice. Join the bodice to the skirt,

Stitch length of bodice trim to the purl ridge marker on the bodice front.

Join shoulder seams.

Stitch each length of cuff lace to cast-on edge of each sleeve. Join sleeve underarm seams, and stitch sleeves into place.

Starting at the hem, join the centre-back seam on each skirt layer to within about 1cm (⅜in) of the waistline.

Put the dress onto the doll, and complete the skirt and bodice back seam.

Starting and ending at the centre-front, stitch the collar to the neckline and slip-stitch the edges of the bodice lace to the armhole/sleeve seam.

If necessary, run a gathering thread round the waist of the dress and draw up tightly before fitting the belt.

Place a small bow on centre front of belt.

Goodnight

Changes in style and shape have always developed more slowly in nightwear than in daywear, and the Edwardian experience was no exception. Although the new pyjamas were now available for both men and women, they were not popular. The bedtime garments worn by most Edwardian families were very similar in shape and style to those that had been worn by their Victorian

'Two or three dozen nightdresses are not too many. Americans and other ultra-smart folk are very fond of black silk or gauze nightgowns, but I do not think they should have a place in bridal trousseaux'

The Lady's Realm, 1903

grandparents. The nightdress still covered the body from chin to ankle (it was floor length, high necked and long sleeved), but now it was much more elaborately trimmed, with lots of lace and ribbon decoration, and it was also made from finer, more luxurious fabrics.

Most men still preferred a long nightshirt made from cotton, natural wool or striped flannelette, but others took to the new pyjamas made from cotton or silk. Even though many homes were now better heated, many people maintained the custom of covering the head during the night. The more elderly ladies still

Preparing for bed: actresses from a production of the musical play 'The Little Michus', c. 1905.

wore the traditional mob cap, which had ties under the chin, but the shape was beginning to change. The modern women wore a cap that was shaped almost like a bathing cap, sitting to the back of the head rather than on top. As for male headwear, high fashion or not, many an elderly gentlemen could still be found wearing his 'Wee Willy Winkie' hat.

It was not until the end of the decade that major changes took place. The mood of the relaxed, less formal, less structured late afternoon-tea period began to be repeated in the private, after-dinner, before-bed period. This was the time for mulling over the events of the day, wearing a night-gown not too dissimilar to the tea-gown – but now the neckline was getting lower and short sleeves were gaining popularity. The short jacket or bolero that was sometimes worn over the tea-gown in the afternoons became long, fussy, frilly and very feminine for bedroom wear – the fore-runner of what we would call a negligée.

Well, it's almost time to say goodnight: father is nice and cosy in his nightshirt and nightcap, and mother is wearing her lace-decorated nightdress with a matching mob cap. The family is ready for bed.

NIGHTSHIRT AND NIGHTCAP

Materials
- A pair each of size 20 and size 21 needles
- 100 reel of Gütermann pure silk S303, in cream (col 802)
- Four tiny beads or buttons

Tension
9sts and 11 rows equal 1cm (⅜in), using size 20 needles over st st

NIGHTSHIRT

BACK
*Using size 21 needles, cast on 50sts and k 2 rows,
Change to size 20 needles and k 1 row,
Shape hem
Next row: k to last 4sts, turn,
Next row: sl1, p to last 4sts, turn,
Next row: sl1, k38, turn,
Next row: sl1, p35, turn,
Next row: sl1, k32, turn,
Cont in this way working 3sts less on each row, until you have worked the row (sl1, k17), then turn and k to end,
Next row: k2, p to last 2sts, k2*,
Next row: k to end
Next row: k2, p to last 2sts, k2
Rep the last 2 rows, 8 times more.
Next row: k to end,
Next row: p to end
Work a further 76 rows in st st as now set,
Shape armholes
Cast off 2sts at the beg of the next 2 rows, then dec 1 st at each end of the next 2 rows,
Cont in st st without shaping for 21 rows, to finish with a RS row,
Shape shoulders
Next row: p36, turn,
Next row: sl1, k6, cast off 16, k the next 6sts, turn,
Next row: sl1, p4, p2tog, turn,
Cast off 12sts.
Return to rem sts with WS facing rejoin yarn, p2tog, then p to end,
Cast off.

FRONT
Follow the instruction for the back from * to *
Next row: k to end
Next row: k2, p to last 2sts, k2,
Rep the last 2 rows, 5 more times,
Beg with a k row work 74 rows in st st
Divide front for neck opening
Next row: k27, turn, k4, p to end,
Cont to work on these sts only to complete L front,
Next row: k to end
Next row: k4, p to end,
Next row: cast off 2, k the next 21sts, yfwd, k2tog, k1
Next row: k4, p to last 2sts, p2tog,
Next row: k2tog, k to end,
Next row: k4, p to end,
Cont without shaping, keeping the 4 garter sts as set, but work a button hole on the 3rd row, and the [foll 6th row] twice, then work 4 rows straight to finish at the neck edge,
Shape neck and shoulders
Next row: cast off 8sts, p to end,
Next row: k,
Next row: cast off 3, p the next 5, turn,
Next row: sl1, k5, turn,
Next row: sl1, p to end,
Cast off.

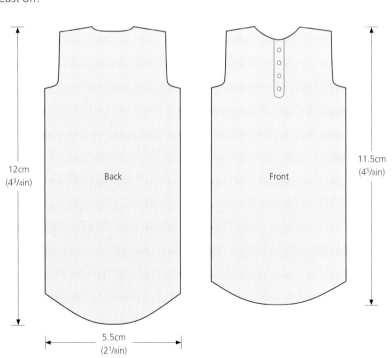

12cm (4¾in)

Back

Front

11.5cm (4⅝in)

5.5cm (2⅛in)

Right front

Return to rem sts with RS facing, rejoin yarn, cast on 4sts and k to end,

Next row: p to last 4sts, k4,

Cont in patt as set for 3 rows,

Shape armholes

Cast off 2 sts at beg of next row, then dec 1 st at the armhole end of the next 2 rows,

Work straight for 20 rows,

Shape neck and shoulders

Next row: cast off 8, k to end,

Next row: p,

Next row: cast off 3, k the next 5, turn,

Next row: sl1, p5,

Cast off.

SLEEVES

Using size 21 needles cast on 28sts, work in k1, p1, rib for 6 rows,

Change to size 20 needles, work in st st and shape the sides as follows.

Inc 1st at each end of the next row, then each end of every foll 6th row, until there are 40sts,

Work 7 rows straight,

Shape top

Cast off 2sts at the beg of the next 4 rows, then

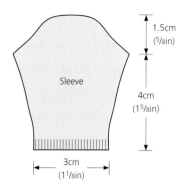

Sleeve

1.5cm (⁵⁄₈in)

4cm (1⁵⁄₈in)

3cm (1¹⁄₈in)

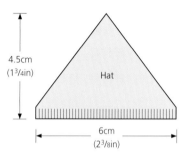

Hat

4.5cm (1³⁄₄in)

6cm (2³⁄₈in)

dec 1 st at each end of the next 6 RS rows, (20sts), then dec 1st at each end of the next 5 rows,

Cast off rem 10sts.

Work a second sleeve to match.

NECK BAND

Using size 21 needles, cast on 44sts, then cast them off.

NIGHTCAP

Using size 21 needles cast on 55sts, and work 6 rows of k1, p1, rib,

Change to size 20 needles, beg with a k row work 4 rows st st,

Shape point

1st row: [k2tog, k9] to end,

2nd and all alt rows: p

3rd row: k,

5th row: [k2tog, k8] to end,

7th row: k,

8th row: p

Cont. to dec in this way on the next row, and every foll 4th row, until there are 5sts,

Next row: k2tog, k1, k2tog,

Next row: p3tog,

Fasten off.

TO MAKE UP

Bag out, block and steam the pieces following the instructions in the section on finishing (page 6).

Shirt. Fold the L front buttonhole band over the R front band, and slip st the cast-off sts to the underside, stitch on beads or buttons to match buttonholes.

Join shoulder seams.

Place the cast-on edge of the neck-band to the neckline, begin at the outside corner of the L front, stitch together for 2sts, then miss 2sts, to make a buttonhole, continue to stitch the band to the neckline, finishing at the outside corner of the R front. Steam the band so that it stands up slightly with the cast-off edge towards the face. Stitch on button to match the buttonhole.

Join side seams, working from the top of the garter stitch edge to the armhole, leaving a slit at the hem edge.

Join each sleeve underarm seam, stitch the sleeves into place.

Cap. Join seam.

NIGHTDRESS AND MOB CAP

The main body of this lady's nightdress is knitted in one piece. Knitting begins at the front hem, working up to the shoulders and then down the back to finish at the back hem.

To help the accurate placement of the lace trim, purl ridge rows are knitted on the right side of the garment and the lace is stitched to these ridges. The lace inset on the bodice is also edged with a narrow trim.

Materials

● A pair each of size 21, and size 20 needles,
● 100m reel of Gütermann pure silk S303 in white, (col 800)

Tension

9sts and 11 rows equal 1cm (⅜in), using size 20 needles over st st

Abbreviations

sl2tog-k1-p2sso: place the point of the right hand needle into the next 2sts as if to k2tog, but do not work them, instead slip both sts onto the right hand needle, k the next st and pass the 2 slipped sts over this st and off the needle
2yo: wrap the yarn twice round the needle to make 2 new sts

HEM LACE

Using size 21 needles, cast on 3 sts and k1 row.
1st row: k1, 2yfwd, k2tog,
2nd row: yfwd, k2, p1, k1,
3rd and 4th row: k5,
5th row: k1, [2yfwd, k2tog,] twice,
6th row: [k2, p1] twice, k1
7th and 8th row: k7
9th row: k1, [2yfwd, k2tog], 3 times
10th row: [k2, p1] 3 times, k1,
11th row: k10,
12th row: Cast off 7sts k to end.
These 12 rows, form the patt and are repeated.

SLEEVE LACE

Using size 21 needles, cast on 3sts, and k 1 row,
1st row: k1, yfwd, yrn, k2tog,
2nd row: yfwd, k2, p1, k1,
3rd and 4th rows: k5,

5th row: k1, [yfwd, yrn, k2tog] twice,
6th row: [k2, p1] twice, k1,
7th row: k7,
8th row: cast off 4sts, k to end.
These 8 rows form the patt and are repeated.

BODICE LACE

Using size 21 needles, cast on 3sts and k 2 rows,
1st and 2nd rows: sl1, k2,
3rd row: sl1, k1, yfwd, k fbf,,
4th row: cast off 3sts, k to end,
These 4 rows form the patt and are repeated.

NIGHTGOWN

FRONT

Using size 20 needles, cast on 87sts
* Beg with a k row, and work 4 rows in st st
dec 1 st at each end of the next row and the foll 6th row,

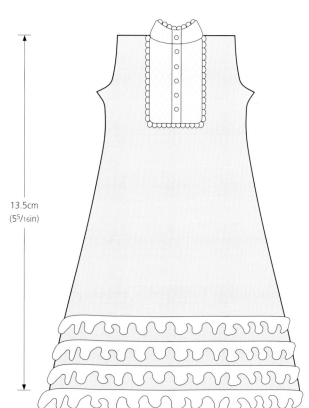

13.5cm
(5⁵⁄₁₆in)

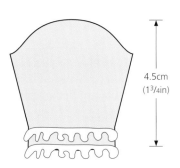

4.5cm
(1³/₄in)

Next row: (WS), k to end*

Rep from * to * twice more,

Work 4 rows in st st then dec 1 st. at each end of the next row, then [every foll 6th row] until there are 49sts, finish with a WS row.

Next row: k17, p15, k to end,

Divide front bodice

Next row: p26, turn, cont on these sts only, leaving rem sts on a spare needle.

1st row: k3, yfwd, ssk, k1, k2tog, yfwd, k to end,

2nd row: p23, k3,

3rd row: k3, yfwd, sl2tog-k1-p2sso, yfwd, k to end

4th row: p23, k1, yfwd, k2tog,

The last 4 rows establish the patt, cont in patt, but **at the same time**, inc 1 st. at the armhole edge of the next 4 rows,

Shape armhole

Keeping lace patt straight, work 1 row,

cast off 2sts at beg of the next row and the foll alt row, now dec 1st at the armhole edge of next 4 rows (22sts)

Work yoke

Next row: k3, yfwd, ssk, k1, k2tog, yfwd, [p1, k1] to end,

Next row: [p1, k1] 7 times, p5, k3,

Next row: k3, yfwd, sl2tog-k1-p2sso, yfwd, [p1, k1] to end,

Next row: [p1, k1] 7 times, p5, k1, yfwd, k2tog,

Shape neck

Cast off 8 sts, rib to end,

Keeping rib straight, dec 1 st at the neck edge of the next 2 rows, then work 3 rows straight. Break off yarn and transfer these 12 sts onto a spare needle.

Return to the left front sts on the spare needle, with WS facing, rejoin yarn,

Cast on 3 sts, p to end,

1st row: k18, yfwd, ssk, k1, k2tog, yfwd, k3

2nd and 4th rows: k3, p to end

3rd row: k18 yfwd, sl2tog-k1-p2sso, yfwd, k3,

These last 4 rows establish the patt, cont in patt but inc1 st at the armhole edge of the next 4 rows,

Shape armhole

Keeping patt straight, cast off 2 sts at the beg of the next row, then foll alt row, patt 1 row, then dec 1 st at the armhole edge of the next 4 rows. (22sts)

Work yoke

Next row: [k1, p1] 7 times, yfwd, ssk, k1, k2tog, yfwd, k3,

Next row: k3, p5, [k1, p1] to end,

Cont in rib patt as now set, for 5 more rows,

Shape neck

Cast off 8 sts, rib to end,

Keeping rib straight, dec 1 st at the neck edge of the next 2 rows, then work 2 rows straight.

Join fronts to work back yoke

Next row: Rib across the left front, turn and cast on 15sts, turn,

Making sure that the RS of each piece is facing, cont in rib across sts from spare needle, (39sts),

Cont in rib as set for 11 more rows,

Shape armholes,

Change to st st, beg with a k row and inc1 st at each end of the next 4 rows, then cast on 2sts at the beg of the foll 4 rows,

Shape waist

Dec1 st at each end of the next 4 rows,

Work 6 rows straight,

Shape back

Inc 1 st at each end of the next row, then every foll 6th row until there are 75sts,

** Work 4 rows straight,

Next row: (WS facing), k, to place marker for the lace trim.

Inc 1 st. at each end of the next row, then the foll

6th row

Rep from ** to ** twice more

Inc 1 st at each end of each foll 6th row until there are 87sts, work 3 more rows. Cast off loosely.

SLEEVES

Using size 20 needles, cast on 30sts,

Beg with a k row and work 4 rows in st st, then inc1 st. at each end of the next row,

Next row: k, (to place marker for attaching lace trim)

Still in st st inc 1 st at each end of foll 5th row, and

then [each foll 6th row] until there are 40sts, work 5 rows straight.

Shape sleeve head
Cast off 2sts at the beg of next 4 rows, then dec1 st at each end of the next row,
p 1 row, then dec1 st at each end of the next 4 rows.
Cast off 4sts at the beg of the next 4 rows,
Cast off rem 6sts.
Work a second sleeve to match.

COLLAR

Using size 21 needles, cast on 7sts, and k 1 row,
Next row: k3, k2tog, yfwd, k2,
Next row: k
Work in patt as folls.
1st row: sl1, k1, yfwd, sl2tog-k1-p2sso, yfwd, k1, k into front, then back, then front, of next st.
2nd row: cast off 2sts, p4, k2,
3rd row: sl1, k1, yfwd, sl2tog-k1-p2sso, yfwd, k2,
4th row: sl1, k1, p3, k2,
Rep these last 4 rows 10 times more, then rows 1 and 2 once, k 3 rows,
Cast off (there should be 12 points).

LACE EDGINGS

The hem of the nightdress is trimmed with 3 rows of the hem lace.
For each row you will need 15 reps of the patt.
Each sleeve is trimmed with 2 rows of the sleeve lace. For each row you will need 5 reps of the patt.
To trim the bodice you will need an 18 repeat length of the bodice lace.

MOB CAP

Using size 20 needles, cast on 120sts
P 1 row.
Next row: [k2tog, k10], rep to end
Next and all alt rows: p
Next row: [k2tog, k9], rep to end,
Next row: [k2tog, k8], rep to end,
Cont to dec in this way until the k2tog, k1, row has been completed,
Next row: [k2tog] to end,
Break off yarn, leaving an end long enough to thread through the rem sts, pull up tightly and fasten off.
Lace brim
Work 18 reps of the sleeve lace.

TO MAKE UP

Bag out, block and steam the pieces following the instructions in the section on finishing (page 6).

Bodice edging. With the right side of the narrow bodice trim uppermost, match the centre of the straight edge of the trim to the centre of the purl ridge at the base of the bodice lace panel. Tack or pin the trim along the ridge and up each side of the lace panel, finishing at the neckline. Very carefully stitch the trim in place, using tiny sts. On the inside of the nightgown, catch down the button band cast-on sts.

Collar. Fold the collar in half lengthwise, and mark the centre. With right sides together, match the collar centre mark to the centre-back neck of nightdress. Very carefully over-sew the straight edge of the collar to the neckline. Fold the collar up, so that it will fit like a band round the neck. Stitch tiny beads or buttons onto the button band.

Gather the sleeve head to fit the armhole and stitch the sleeves into place. With the sleeves in place, stitch each side seam, working from sleeve cuff to gown hem.

Hem trims. Join each length of nightgown trim into a circle. With right sides together over-sew one length round the hem edge of the gown, and the remaining lengths to the purl ridge markers, gathering the lace slightly as necessary.

Sleeve trim. Join each length of sleeve trim into a circle. With RS together over-sew a length of sleeve trim to the cast-on edge of the sleeve, and a second length to the purl ridge marker.

Mob cap. With right sides together, stitch the seam from cast-on edge to gather point.

Join the trim into a circle. With right sides together, stitch the straight edge of trim to the cast-on edge of cap gathering to fit. Run a gathering thread of fine shirring elastic around the cast on edge of the cap, and draw up to fit.

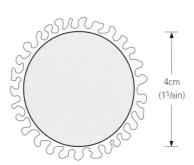

4cm
(1⁵/₈in)

GIRL'S NIGHTDRESS AND MOB CAP

Materials
- A pair of size 20 needles
- 100m reel of Gütermann pure silk S303, in white (col 800)
- Three tiny beads or buttons for front fastening

Tension
9sts and 11 rows equal 1cm (⅜in), using size 20 needles over st st

Abbreviations
ssk, [slip 1 st knitwise] twice, then approaching from the left, insert the point of the LH needle into the front of these 2sts, and then knit them tog from this position.

sl1-k2tog-psso, slip the next stitch, k2tog, pass the slipped stitch over and off the needle

LACE PATTERN
Cast on 4sts and k 1 row,
1st row: k2, yfwd, k2,

2nd row: k2, yfwd, k1, yfwd, k2,
3rd row: k2, yfwd, k3, yfwd, k2,
4th row: k2, yfwd, k5, yfwd, k2,
5th row: k2, yfwd, ssk, k3, k2tog, yfwd, k2,
6th row: k3, yfwd, ssk, k1, k2tog, yfwd, k3,
7th row: k4, yfwd, sl1-k2tog-psso, yfwd, k4,
8th row: cast off 7sts, k3, (4sts)
These 8 rows form the pattern and are repeated.

SMALL LACE PATTERN
Using size 20 needles, cast on 4sts,
1st row: k1, p3,
2nd row: k1, yfwd, k1 tbl, yfwd, sl1-k1-psso,
3rd row: k1, p2, [k1, p1, k1, p1] into next st, p1,
4th row: cast off 4, k the next st, yfwd, sl1-k1-psso,
These 4 rows form the pattern and are repeated.

NIGHTDRESS

BACK
Using size 20 needles cast on 50sts, and p 1 row,
Next row: k37, turn,
Next row: sl1, p23, turn,
Next row: sl1, k to end,
Next row: p,
Work 2 rows in st st, then dec 1 st at each end of the next row,
Work 4 rows straight, then k the next row.
Beg with a k row, cont in st st, but shape sides by dec 1 st at each end of the next row, then each end of [the foll 6th row] twice, and [foll 4th row] 6 times, (30sts)
Work 3 rows straight.
Shape armholes
Cast off 2sts at the beg of the next 2 rows, and dec 1st at each end of the foll row**
Work 16 rows straight.
Shape shoulders and neck
Next row: p 20, turn,
Next row: sl1, k15, turn,
Next row: sl1, p3, cast off 8, p to end,
Cast off 8sts and break off yarn,
Rejoin yarn to rem 8sts and cast them off.

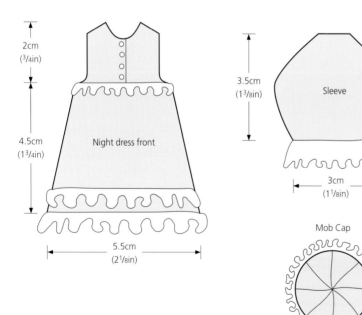

2cm
(¾in)

4.5cm
(1¾in)

Night dress front

5.5cm
(2⅛in)

3.5cm
(1⅜in)

Sleeve

3cm
(1⅛in)

Mob Cap

3cm
(1⅛in)

FRONT

Foll instructions for the back until ** is reached, k the next 2 rows,

Divide to work right front
Next row: p11, k2, turn,
Next row: k to end,
Next row: p11 k2,
Rep the last 2 rows, 4 more times,

Shape neck
Next row: cast off 2sts, k to end,
Next row: p9, p2tog,
Next row: k2tog, k to end,
Next row: p7, p2tog,
Next row: k4, turn,
Next row: sl1, p3,
Cast off the rem 8sts.

Work left front
With the WS facing, return to the rem sts, and rejoin yarn,
Cast on 2 sts, k2, p to end,
Next row: k,
Next row: k2, p to end,
In patt as now set work 7 rows,
Next row: cast off 2sts, p to end,
Work 1 row,
Dec 1 st at the neck edge of the next 2 rows,

Shape shoulder
Next row: p2tog, p3, turn,
Next row: sl1, k3,
Next row: p8,
Cast off.

SLEEVES

Using size 20 needles cast on 24sts, and p 1 row,
Beg with a k row work in st st, and inc 1 st at each end of the 3rd row, then every foll 4th row until there are 36sts.

Shape top
Dec 1 st at each end of every row, until there are 8sts left,
Cast off.

BODICE LACE

Work 5 repeats of the Small Lace pattern.

HEM LACE

Work 2 lengths of the Hem Lace Pattern, each to be 16 repeats long.

SLEEVE LACE

Work 6 repeats of the Small Lace Pattern for each sleeve.

COLLAR

Work 6 reps of the Small Lace Pattern.

MOB CAP

Using size 20 needles cast on 80sts and p 1 row,
1st row: [k2tog, k8] rep to end,
Next and all alt rows: p
3rd row: [k2tog, k7] rep to end,
5th row: [k2tog, k6] rep to end,
Cont to dec on each alt row as set, until there are 16sts left, finish with a p row,
Next 2 rows: [k2tog] to end,
Break off yarn and thread through rem sts, pull up tightly and fasten off.

LACE EDGING

Work 19 repeats of the Small Lace Pattern.

TO MAKE UP

Bag out, block and steam the pieces following the instructions in the section on finishing (page 6).

Slightly gather the length of bodice lace and slip-stitch to the marker ridge on the bodice.

Fold the button band under the buttonhole band and secure the cast-on stitches to the underside.

Join shoulder and side seams of the nightdress. Stitch one length of hem lace to the bottom edge of nightdress and the second length to the marker ridge.

Stitch a length of sleeve lace to each sleeve end. Join the sleeve seams, and stitch sleeves into place.

Stitch the collar into place, starting and finishing at the centre of each front band.

Add buttons to front button band.

Stitch the lace to the cast-on edge of the cap. Join the seam from the gathered point to lace edging.

Run a gathering thread of very fine elastic along the cast-on edge above the lace. Pull up to fit, and fasten off.

BOY'S NIGHTSHIRT AND CAP

Materials
- A pair each of size 20 and size 21 needles
- 100m reel of Gütermann pure silk S303, in cream (col 802)
- Tiny beads or buttons for front fastening

Tension
9sts and 11 rows equal 1cm (⅜in), using size 20 needles over st st

BACK
Using size 20 needles cast on 33sts and k 3 rows,
Next row: k22sts, turn,
Next row: sl1, p10, turn,
Next row: sl1, k13, turn,
Next row: sl1, p16, turn,
Next row: sl1, k19, turn,
Next row: sl1, p22, turn,
Next row: sl1, k25, turn,
Next row: sl1, p28, turn,
Next row: sl1, k30, turn,
Next row: k2, p to last 2sts, k2,
Next row: k to end,
Next row: k2, p to last 2 sts k2,
Rep the last 2 rows twice more.
Change to st st, beg with a RS row, cast on 1 st at the beg of the next 2 rows,
Work 32 rows,
Shape armholes
Cast off 2sts at the beg of the next 2 rows **, then dec 1 st at each end of the foll 3 rows, work straight for 22 rows,
Shape shoulders and neck
Next row: p21, turn,
Next row: sl1, k16, turn,
Next row: p to end,
Cast off.

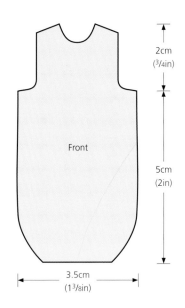

Front

2cm (¾in)

5cm (2in)

3.5cm (1³⁄₈in)

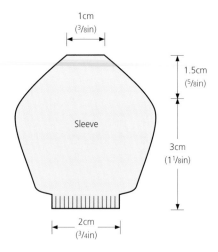

1cm (³⁄₈in)

Sleeve

1.5cm (⁵⁄₈in)

3cm (1¹⁄₈in)

2cm (¾in)

FRONT
Foll the instructions for the back until ** is reached.
Dec 1 st at each end of the next 2 rows,
Divide front
Next row: k2tog, k13, turn,
Next row: k3, p to end,
Cont on these 14sts only to complete the L front,

Next row: k,
Next row: k3, p to end,
rep the last 2 rows once more,
Next row: k to last 3sts, yfwd, k2tog, k1,
Work 6 rows straight,
Next row: k1, k2tog, yfwd, p to end,
Work 6 rows straight,
Next row: k to last 3sts, yfwd, k2tog, k1,
Shape neck

Cast off 3sts, p to end,
Next row: k,
Next row: p2tog, p5, turn,
Next row: k4, k2tog,
Next row: p2tog, p to end,
Cast off.
Work right front
Return to rem sts with RS facing, rejoin yarn, cast on 3sts and k to end,
Next row: p to last 3 sts, k3,
Next row: k,
Next row: p to last 3sts, k3,
Rep the last 2 rows 9 more times
Shape neck and shoulder
Cast off 3sts at beg of next row, and dec 1 st at the end of foll row,
Next row: k2tog, k4, turn,
Next row: sl1, p2, p2tog,
Cast off.

SLEEVES

Using size 21 needles cast on 18sts, and work 6 rows in k1, p1, rib
Change to size 20 needles,
Inc row: k4, [k twice into the next st] 10 times, k4, (28sts)
Next row: p to end,
Cont in st st, but shape sides by inc 1 st at each end of the 3rd row, then each end of [the foll 6th row] 3 times,
Work three rows straight, (36sts)
Shape top
Dec 1 st at each end of every row until there are 8sts left, cast off.
Work a second sleeve to match.

COLLAR

Using size 21 needles, cast on 27sts, then cast them off again.

NIGHTCAP

Using size 21 needles cast on 45sts and work 4 rows in k1, p1, rib,
Change to size 20 needles, beg with a k row work 4 rows st st,
Shape point
1st row: [k2tog, k7] to end,
2nd and all alt rows: p,
3rd row: k,

5th row: [k2tog, k6] to end,
7th row: k,
8th row: p,
Cont to dec in this way on the next row, then every foll 4th row, until there are 5sts,
Next row: p to end,
Next row: k2tog, k1, k2tog,
Next row: p3tog,
Fasten off.

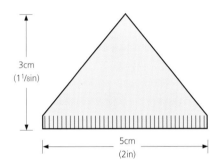

3cm (1 1/8in)

5cm (2in)

TO MAKE UP

Bag out, block and steam the pieces following the instructions in the section on finishing (page 6).

Nightshirt. Slip stitch the cast-on sts of the button band to the under side of the buttonhole band.

Join front and back shoulder seams.

Join side seams, from armhole to the top of the garter stitch edge, so that the shirt has short slits at the side.

Stitch the cast-off edge of the collar to the neckline, so that the cast-on edge is towards the face.

Join the underarm seams of the sleeves and stitch the sleeves into place.

Stitch on beads or buttons to match the buttonholes.

Nightcap. Join seam from point to cast-on edge.

FURTHER READING

GENERAL FASHION

Bond, David. *The Guinness Guide to 20th Century Fashion*, (Guinness Superlative, 1981)

Byrde, Penelope. *A Visual History of Costume, 20C*, (B. T. Batsford, 1986)

Carter, Ernestine. *The Changing World of Fashion*, (Butler and Tanner Ltd, 1977)

Cunnington, Phillis. *English Costume for Sports and Outdoor Recreation*, (A. C. Black Ltd, 1969)

Ewing, Elizabeth, *History of 20C Fashion*, (B. T. Batsford, 1974)

Gernsheim, Alison. *Victorian and Edwardian Fashion*, (Dover, 1963)

Laver, James. *Costume through the Ages*, (Thames and Hudson, 1964)

Peacock, John. *Costume 1066-1966*, (Thames and Hudson, 1986)

Stevenson, Pauline, *Edwardian Fashion*, (Ian Allen Ltd, 1980)

Yarwood, Doreen, *Fashion in the Western World*, (B. T. Batsford, 1992)

FASHION FOR MEN

De Marley, Diana. *Fashion for Men, An Illustrated History*, (B.T. Batsford, 1985)

Sichel, Marion. *History of Men's Costume*, (B. T. Batsford, 1984)

Waugh, Nora. *The Cut of Men's Clothes, 1600-1900*, (Faber and Faber, 1964)

HISTORY OF UNDERWEAR

Ewing, Elizabeth. *Dress and Undress*, (Anchor Brendon Ltd, 1978)

Ewing, Elizabeth. *Fashion in Underwear*, (B.T.Batsford, 1971)

Farrel, Jeremy. *Socks and Stockings*, (B. T. Batsford, 1992)

Willett,C. and Cunnington, Phillis. *The History of Underclothes*, (Faber and Faber, 1981)

HISTORY OF CHILDREN'S FASHION

Clare, Rose. *Children's Clothes*, (B. T. Batsford, 1989)

Cunnington and Buck. *Children's Costume in England, 1300-1900*, (A. C. Black, 1965)

Davidson, Alexander. *Blazers, Badges and Boaters*, (Scope Books Ltd, 1990)

Ewing, Elizabeth. *History of Children's Costume*, (B. T. Batsford, 1977)

ACCESSORIES

Cumming, Valerie. *The Visual History of Costume Accessories*, (Routledge, 1998)

Farrell, Jeremy. *Umbrellas and Parasols*, (B. T. Batsford, 1985)

Farrell, Jeremy, *Socks and Stockings*, (B. T. Batsford, 1992)

Foster, Vanda. *Bags and Purses*, (B. T. Batsford, 1982)

Felkin, William. *Felkins History of the Machine Wrought Hosiery and Lace Industry*, (David and Charles, 1967)

USEFUL ADDRESSES

While readers in Britain should have no trouble finding the needle sizes used in this book, there are no American equivalents for British sizes 20 and 21 and there is no equivalent for size 21 in continental Europe. The two companies below sell the complete range of mini knitting pins.

MINIATURE KNITTING AND RUG SUPPLIES

14, Woodbank Drive
Brandlesholme,
Bury, Lancashire, UK
BL8 1DR
Tel: 0161 797 7983
www.minknit.freeserve.co.uk
[This company sells its whole range on-line]

MEADOWCROFT MINIATURES

Bossiney Road,
Tintagel,
Cornwall, UK
PL34 0AB
Tel: 01840 770613
www.meadowcroft-min.co.uk
[No on-line buying facility]

About the Author

Yvonne Wakefield is a fashion designer who for many years marketed her own label collection in America and Japan as well as freelancing for a variety of clients. Her design work during this period included knitwear for Ralph Lauren's Polo range and his New York runway shows. She later lectured in fashion design and marketing at De Montfort University in Lincoln, England, where she managed the fashion department.

Her design work, including knitting designs and instructions, has been published in many periodicals and in pattern leaflet form for several of the leading yarn manufacturers.

She was attracted to the world of miniatures by the challenge of adapting her practical skills and her knowledge of fashion to an ancient hand craft using basic, unsophisticated equipment. This is her first book.

Index

Page numbers for knitting patterns are highlighted in **bold**.

GMC TITLES

WOODCARVING

The Art of the Woodcarver ....GMC Publications
Beginning Woodcarving.................................GMC Publications
Carving Architectural Detail in Wood:
  The Classical Tradition ....Frederick Wilbur
Carving Birds & Beasts ....GMC Publications
Carving the Human Figure:
  Studies in Wood and Stone ....Dick Onians
Carving Nature: Wildlife Studies in Wood......Frank Fox-Wilson
Carving Realistic Birds..David Tippey
Decorative Woodcarving...................................Jeremy Williams
Elements of Woodcarving...Chris Pye
Essential Woodcarving Techniques ....Dick Onians
Lettercarving in Wood: A Practical Course ....Chris Pye
Making & Using Working Drawings
  for Realistic Model Animals............................Basil F. Fordham
Power Tools for Woodcarving...............................David Tippey
Relief Carving in Wood: A Practical Introduction.........Chris Pye
Understanding Woodcarving ....GMC Publications
Understanding Woodcarving in the Round ....GMC Publications
Useful Techniques for Woodcarvers ....GMC Publications
Wildfowl Carving – Volume 1 ....Jim Pearce
Wildfowl Carving – Volume 2 ....Jim Pearce
Woodcarving: A Complete Course ....Ron Butterfield
Woodcarving: A Foundation Course.......................Zoë Gertner
Woodcarving for Beginners ....GMC Publications
Woodcarving Tools & Equipment
  Test Reports ....GMC Publications
Woodcarving Tools, Materials & Equipment ....Chris Pye

WOODTURNING

Adventures in Woodturning.................................David Springett
Bert Marsh: Woodturner ....Bert Marsh
Bowl Turning Techniques Masterclass ....Tony Boase
Colouring Techniques for Woodturners ....Jan Sanders
Contemporary Turned Wood: New Perspectives in
  a Rich Tradition ....Ray Leier, Jan Peters & Kevin Wallace
The Craftsman Woodturner ....Peter Child
Decorating Turned Wood:
The Maker's Eye ....Liz & Michael O'Donnell
Decorative Techniques for Woodturners................Hilary Bowen
Fun at the Lathe ....R.C. Bell
Illustrated Woodturning Techniques ....John Hunnex
Intermediate Woodturning Projects ....GMC Publications
Keith Rowley's Woodturning Projects ....Keith Rowley
Making Screw Threads in Wood ....Fred Holder
Turned Boxes: 50 Designs..Chris Stott
Turning Green Wood ....Michael O'Donnell
Turning Miniatures in Wood..............................John Sainsbury
Turning Pens and Pencils....Kip Christensen & Rex Burningham
Understanding Woodturning ....Ann & Bob Phillips

Useful Techniques for Woodturners ....GMC Publications
Useful Woodturning Projects ....GMC Publications
Woodturning: Bowls, Platters, Hollow Forms, Vases,
  Vessels, Bottles, Flasks, Tankards, Plates.......GMC Publications
Woodturning: A Foundation Course
  (New Edition)..Keith Rowley
Woodturning: A Fresh Approach ....Robert Chapman
Woodturning: An Individual Approach ....Dave Regester
Woodturning: A Source Book of Shapes ....John Hunnex
Woodturning Jewellery ....Hilary Bowen
Woodturning Masterclass ....Tony Boase
Woodturning Techniques................................GMC Publications
Woodturning Tools & Equipment
  Test Reports ....GMC Publications
Woodturning Wizardry.......................................David Springett

WOODWORKING

Advanced Scrollsaw Projects ....GMC Publications
Beginning Picture Marquetry ....Lawrence Threadgold
Bird Boxes and Feeders for the Garden.............Dave Mackenzie
Complete Woodfinishing ....Ian Hosker
David Charlesworth's Furniture-Making
  Techniques...David Charlesworth
David Charlesworth's Furniture-Making
  Techniques – Volume 2 ....David Charlesworth
The Encyclopedia of Joint Making ....Terrie Noll
Furniture-Making Projects for the
  Wood Craftsman ....GMC Publications
Furniture-Making Techniques for
  the Wood Craftsman ....GMC Publications
Furniture Projects...Rod Wales
Furniture Restoration (Practical Crafts) ....Kevin Jan Bonner
Furniture Restoration: A Professional at Work...........John Lloyd
Furniture Restoration and Repair
  for Beginners..Kevin Jan Bonner
Furniture Restoration Workshop.....................Kevin Jan Bonner
Green Woodwork ....Mike Abbott
The History of Furniture ....Michael Huntley
Intarsia: 30 Patterns for the Scrollsaw.....................John Everett
Kevin Ley's Furniture Projects...................................Kevin Ley
Making & Modifying Woodworking Tools ....Jim Kingshott
Making Chairs and Tables.............................GMC Publications
Making Chairs and Tables – Volume 2............GMC Publications
Making Classic English Furniture.......................Paul Richardson
Making Heirloom Boxes ....Peter Lloyd
Making Little Boxes from Wood ....John Bennett
Making Screw Threads in Wood ....Fred Holder
Making Shaker Furniture ....Barry Jackson
Making Woodwork Aids and Devices................Robert Wearing
Mastering the Router...Ron Fox
Minidrill: Fifteen Projects.......................................John Everett
Pine Furniture Projects for the Home ....Dave Mackenzie
Practical Scrollsaw Patterns ....John Everett
Router Magic: Jigs, Fixtures and Tricks to
  Unleash your Router's Full Potential ....Bill Hylton
Router Tips & Techniques ....GMC Publications
Routing: A Workshop Handbook.......................Anthony Bailey

UPHOLSTERY

TOYMAKING

DOLLS' HOUSES AND MINIATURES

CRAFTS

GARDENING

PHOTOGRAPHY

VIDEOS

MAGAZINES

◆ Woodturning ◆ Woodcarving ◆ Furniture & Cabinetmaking
◆ The Router ◆ Woodworking ◆ The Dolls' House Magazine
◆ Water Gardening ◆ Outdoor Photography
◆ Black & White Photography ◆ BusinessMatters

The above represents a full list of all titles currently published
or scheduled to be published. All are available direct from the
Publishers or through bookshops, newsagents and specialist
retailers. To place an order, or to obtain a complete catalogue,
contact:

GMC Publications,
Castle Place, 166 High Street, Lewes,
East Sussex BN7 1XU, United Kingdom
Tel: 01273 488005 Fax: 01273 478606
E-mail: pubs@thegmcgroup.com
Orders by credit card are accepted